From Marxism to Post-Marxism?

From Marxism

to

Post-Marxism?

GÖRAN THERBORN

VERSO

London • New York

First published by Verso 2008
© Göran Therborn 2008
All rights reserved

The moral rights of the author have been asserted

1 3 5 7 9 10 8 6 4 2

Verso
UK: 6 Meard Street, London W1F 0EG
USA: 20 Jay Street, Suite 1010, Brooklyn, NY 11201
www.versobooks.com

Verso is the imprint of New Left Books

ISBN-13: 978-1-84467-188-5

British Library Cataloguing in Publication Data
A catalogue record for this book is available from the British Library

Library of Congress Cataloging-in-Publication Data
A catalog record for this book is available from the Library of Congress

Typeset by Hewer Text UK Ltd, Edinburgh
Printed in the USA by Maple Vail

Contents

Our Time and the Age of Marx

Karl Marx, born in 1818, is about the same age as Latin American independence. The first calls for independence were issued in 1810, although the decisive anticolonial battles of Mexico and Peru were fought in the 1820s. In Latin America, preparations for bicentenary celebrations in 2010 have already begun. Marx is of course younger than the protagonists of the Latin American liberation struggles – younger than, for instance, the Liberator himself, Simón Bolívar, recently revived as the spiritual guide of the revolution in Venezuela – for he was born in the dark years of European reaction, of the Holy Alliance of counter-revolution. But the seeds of modernity had been deeply planted in the economic and the cultural soil of Western Europe, and Karl witnessed their first flowering. *The Communist Manifesto* appeared – much ahead of its time, with its vision of globalized capitalism and working-class struggles – during 'the Springtide of peoples', the February–March revolutions of 1848.

In terms of his literary counterparts, Marx is much younger than, say, Rumi, Dante, Cervantes or Shakespeare, and as a social and political theorist younger than, for instance, Hobbes and Locke – who in his day were the heroes of Cambridge academic politics – not to speak of classical sages such as Plato, Aristotle, Confucius and Mencius.

Nowadays, it is much harder to determine how long an intellectual will last than to predict the likely lifespan of the average human being. What can we say of Marx's ability to endure? As we approach the bicentennial of the man's birth, is the body of work that bears his name (long?) dead, dying, ageing, or maturing? Is its resurrection possible? Certainly, it would be impossible to argue that the founder of historical materialism is timeless or eternally young.

Any appropriate response would have to take into account the fact that Marx was a great articulator and a multi-dimensional personality. He was an intellectual, a social philosopher of the radical Enlightenment, a social scientist-cum-historian, and a political strategist and leader – first of the diasporic Communist League and then of the International Working Men's Association. Over the decades, these multiple personae have been assigned vastly different meanings and implications. Politics is inescapably a central piece of the legacy of Marxism, but nobody has ever claimed that Marx was a major political leader. He has served as a source of political inspiration and as a social compass for political navigation, but Marx the politician is long dead. Few, if any, social scientists and historians would deny that social and historical methodology, understanding and knowledge have progressed in the 125-odd years since Marx's final illness put an end to his work on the manuscript of *Capital*. But here matters are more complicated, because social analysis, contemporary as well as historical, continues to draw upon 'classics', not only for inspiration but also for topics of research, concepts, interesting aperçus and intriguing insights. Emile Durkheim, Alexis de Tocqueville and Max Weber are coeval classics in this sense, as are Ibn Khaldoun and Machiavelli, although several centuries older. And great philosophers never die – they have their periods of hibernation as well as of flowering, which usually last a stretch of time somewhere between that of Kondratiev cycles and climatic epochs.

This book is more concerned with Marx-*ism* than with

Marx. But as far as Marx in our time is concerned, my impression is that he is maturing, a bit like a good cheese or a vintage wine – not suitable for dionysiac parties or quick gulps at the battlefront. Rather, he is a stimulating companion for profound thought about the meanings of modernity and of human emancipation.

For his forthcoming bicentenary, I would propose three toasts. First, to Karl Marx as a proponent of emancipatory reason, of a rationalist scrutiny of the world, with a commitment to human freedom from exploitation and oppression. Second, to his historical materialist approach to social analysis – in other words, to his understanding of the present as history, with particular attention paid to the living and working conditions of ordinary people and to the economic and political materiality of power – an approach not to be followed as if laid out in a manual, but rather as a broad directive accompanied by the motivation to pursue it further. Third, Karl should be celebrated for his dialectical openness – his sensitivity to, and comprehension of, contradictions, antimonies and conflicts in social life.

Marx-*ism* has, I think, an uncertain future, for reasons explained below. But Marx himself is bound for the long life of alternating winters, springs, summers and autumns undergone by so many of the great thinkers of humankind, from Confucius and Plato onward.

The Nature of this Study

This book is intended as a map and a compass. It is an attempt to understand the seismic social and intellectual shift between the twentieth century – in an important sense the century of Marxism – and the twenty-first century, which began in the years of 1978–91, when China turned to the market and the Soviet system collapsed in both Europe and the USSR itself. It lays no claim to being an intellectual history or a history of ideas, and may be seen rather as a traveller's notebook, unpretentious notes jotted down after a long, arduous journey through the climbs, passes, descents and dead ends of twentieth- and early twenty-first-century Marxism.

The book has two aims. The first is to situate the left-wing political practice and thought of the early twenty-first century in the terrain of the previous century. The second is to provide a systematic panorama of left-wing thought in the North at the beginning of this new century, and to compare it with the Marxism of the preceding era. While abstaining from pleading for any particular path or interpretation, I do not want to hide the fact that this work is written by a scholar who has not surrendered his left-wing commitment. Indeed, it is that very commitment which has motivated the writing of this book.

The two objectives are pursued in three different chapters, of various origins. The first, on the spaces of left-wing thought and practice, was initially presented at a conference in Mexico organized by the senators of the PRD in April 2001, and was then published with a post-September update in *New Left Review* no. 10. Here it has been significantly restructured and rewritten. The second, an attempt at identifying the legacy of twentieth-century Marxism as critical theory, derives from a contribution to the first (1996) edition of Blackwell's *Companion to Social Theory* (edited by Bryan Turner, who also edited the second, twenty-first-century edition). It is here reprinted with minor changes, mainly with a view to avoiding too much overlap with the subsequent essay. The third chapter, on recent radical thought, derives from my contribution to *The Handbook on European Social Theory* (edited by Gerard Delanty for Routledge in 2006), which was later expanded and Atlanticized for publication in *NLR* no. 43. I have updated and somewhat extended it here; some errors – spotted by *NLR* readers and kindly conveyed to me – have been corrected, and some contextual arguments have been moved to other chapters.

As a scholar whose interests are global, I try to situate the Left in global space. But I admit from the outset that a systematic overview of contemporary Southern radical thought has been beyond my linguistic competence as well as my time constraints. I do, nevertheless, take note of the rich legacy of sophisticated left-wing thought in the South, for it is here that the future is likely to be decided.

Cambridge
October–November 2007

Into the Twenty-first Century: The New Parameters of Global Politics

Politics is thought and fought out, policies are forged and implemented, political ideas wax and wane – all within a global space. The space itself decides nothing: only actors and their actions can do that. But it is this dimension – long global, in many respects, but now far denser in its worldwide connectivity – that endows these actors with their strengths and weaknesses, constraints and opportunities. Space provides the coordinates of their political moves. Skill and responsibility in the art of politics, luck and genius – and their opposites – remain constant, but it is the space that largely allocates the political actors their cards.

This global space comprises three major planes. One is socio-economic, laying out the preconditions for the social and economic orientation of politics – in other words, for Left and Right. Another is cultural, with its prevailing patterns of beliefs and identities and the principal means of communication. The third is geopolitical, providing the power parameters for confrontations between and against states. This chapter aims to map the social space of Left–Right politics, from the 1960s to the first decade of the twenty-first century. It is neither a political history nor a strategic programme, although it bears some relevance to both. It is an attempt to assess the strengths and weaknesses of the forces of Left and Right, in a broad, non-partisan sense – both during the recent past, which still bears forcefully on the present, and within emerging currents.

The overall geopolitical space will be invoked only where it most directly affects Left–Right politics. As regards the underlying conceptions, however, a few points of clarification may be needed. The analytical distinction between the two elements does not, of course, imply that they are literally distinct. In the concrete world, social and geopolitical spaces are conjoined. Nevertheless, it is important not to confound the two. The Cold War, for example, had an important Left–Right dimension – that of competing socialist and capitalist modernities. But it also had a specifically geopolitical dynamic, which pitted the two global superpowers against each other and entrained, on each side, allies, clients and friends. Which of these two dimensions was the more important remains a controversial question.

The resources, opportunities and options of interterritorial actors within the geopolitical plane are generated by a variety of factors – military might, demographic weight, economic power and geographical location, among others. For the understanding of Left–Right politics that concerns us here, two further aspects are particularly significant: the distribution of geopolitical power in the world, and the social character of interterritorial, or transterritorial, actors.

On the first, we should note that the distribution of power has changed dramatically during the last forty years, and not just in one direction. The period began with the build-up to the United States' first military defeat in its history, in Vietnam, and with the ascendancy of the USSR to approximate military parity. Then came the collapse of the Soviet Union, and the US claim to a final victory in the Cold War. Although in 1956, the fiasco of the French–British-Israeli invasion of Suez signalled the end of European military might on a world scale, Europe has – as the EU – returned as both an economic great power and a continental laboratory for complex, interstate relations. At the beginning of the period, Japan was the world's rising economic star; currently it is fading economically and rapidly ageing socially. By contrast, China's still unbroken decades of spectacular growth have given economic muscle to its massive demographic weight.

The social character of interterritorial actors can be read not only from the colour of state regimes but also from the orientation and weight of non-state forces. Two new kinds of international actors – of divergent social significance – have become increasingly important during this period.[1] The first consists of transnational interstate organizations such as the World Bank, the IMF and the WTO, which have jointly served as a major neoliberal spearhead for the Right (although the World Bank has had some dissenting voices). The second is a looser set of transnational networks, movements and lobbies for global concerns that have emerged as fairly significant, progressive actors within the world arena – initially through their links with such UN mechanisms as the human rights conventions and major international conferences on women and on population, and, more recently, through their international mobilizations against trade liberalization.

In brief, even though the US has become the only superpower, the geopolitical space has not simply become unipolar; instead, it has begun to assume new forms of complexity.

---

1. Multinational corporations are, of course, an age-old feature of capitalism.

Socio-economic Plane

The social space of modern politics has at least three crucial parameters: states, markets and 'social pattern-ings'.[2] The first two are well-known and highly visible institutional complexes. The third may require some expla-nation. It refers to the shaping of social actors – a process influenced, of course, by states and markets, but with additional force of its own, derived from forms of livelihood and residence, religions and family institutions. It involves not only a class structure but, more fundamentally, a rendering of variable 'classness'. It may be useful here to invoke a more abstract, analytical differentiation of social patterning than the conventional ones of class size or strength, or of categorical identities such as class, gender and ethnicity. The patternings I want to highlight are sociocultural ones, with an emphasis on broad, socially determined cultural orientations rather than just structural categories. Here I suggest irreverence–deference and collectivism–individualism as key dimensions (sketched in Figure 1.1).

Irreverence and deference here refer to orientations towards existing inequalities of power, wealth and status; collectivism and individualism to propensities – high or low – towards collective identification and organization. The classical Left was driven by the 'irreverent collec-tivism' of the socialist working-class and anti-imperialist movements, while other contemporary radical currents – for women's rights or human rights, for instance – have

---

2. Capitalism itself is a system of markets, social patternings and (one or more) states. Looking at the features and, above all, at the interrelationships of these three dimensions is one way – in my experience, a fruitful one – of dissecting power relations and their dynamics within capitalism. These variables have the advantage of opening up into empirical–analytical overviews, while neither presupposing nor requiring assessments of the actual extent of the capitalist 'systemness' of states and social patterns. As current and foreseeable politics can hardly be summed up in terms of socialism vs. capitalism, this conceptual apparatus – broader, looser, less capital/labour-focused – may have some merit.

Figure 1.1: Crucial dimensions of the social patterning of actors

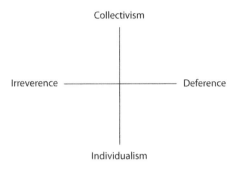

a more individualist character. The traditional Right was institutionally, or clientistically, collectivist; liberalism, both old and new, tends rather towards 'deferential individualism' – deferring to those of supposedly superior status, entrepreneurial bosses, the rich, managers, experts (in particular, liberal economists) – and, at least until recently, male *chefs de famille*, imperial rulers and representatives of *Herrenvolk* empires.

It is within this triangle of states, markets and social patternings that political ideas gain their ascendancy, and political action occurs. The dynamics of this space derive, firstly, from the outcomes of previous political contests; secondly, from the input of new knowledge and technology; and thirdly, from the processes of the economic system – capitalism and, formerly, actually existing socialism. A schematization of the full model is given in Figure 1.2.

COORDINATES OF POLITICAL SPACE

Most contemporary discussions of the state, whether from Left or Right, focus on the question of 'the nation-state' as it confronts globalization, or on privatization as a

Figure 1.2:   Social space of politics and its dynamics

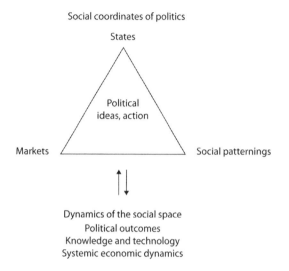

challenge to its institutions. These approaches tend to ignore both the reality of contemporary state policy-making and, even more importantly, the varying structural forms of state development. On the first point, the key question is: has the state's capacity to pursue policy targets actually diminished over the past four decades? The clear answer for developed democracies is that, generally speaking, it has not. On the contrary, one could say that recent years have seen some stunning successes for state policies: the worldwide reduction – indeed, the virtual abolition – of inflation is one major example; the development of strong regional interstate organizations – the EU, ASEAN, Mercosur and NAFTA – is another. True, the persistence of mass unemployment in the EU is a clear policy failure, but the European unemployed have, on the whole, not been pushed into American-style poverty, which must count as at least a modest success.

Policy orientations and priorities have changed; new skills and greater flexibility may be required; as always, a considerable number of policies fail to reach their goals. But this is nothing new. Nation-states, regions and cities will differ, as always, in their effectiveness, but I see no trend towards a generally diminished policy-making capacity. That certain left-wing policies have become more difficult to implement is probably true, but that derives not so much from state-level failures as from the right-wing tilt of the political coordinates.

Successful State Forms

The most serious flaw of conventional globalization discourse, however, is its blindness to the development of strongly differentiated state forms over the past forty years. Two models arose in the sixties: the welfare state, based on generous, publicly financed social entitlements, and the East Asian 'outward development' model. Both have been successfully deployed and consolidated ever since. The core region of welfare statism has been Western Europe, where it has had an impact on all the original OECD countries. Although its European roots go back a long way, it was in the years after 1960 that welfare statism began to soar – in about a decade, the expenditure and revenue of the state suddenly expanded, more than during its entire previous history. Unnoticed by conventional globalization theory, the last four decades of the twentieth century saw the developed states grow at a far greater rate than international trade. For the old OECD as a whole, public expenditure as a proportion of GDP increased by 13 percentage points between 1960 and 1999, while exports grew 11 per cent.[3] For the fifteen

---

3. That is, for the OECD before the recent inclusion of Mexico, South Korea and post-Communist East Central Europe.

members of the European Union, the corresponding figures were 18–19 percentage points and 14 per cent.[4]

Despite the many claims to the contrary – echoed on both Left and Right – the welfare state still stands tall wherever it was constructed. Whether measured by public expenditure or by revenue, the public sector in the richest countries of the world stands at, or has plateaued at, peak historical levels. For the OECD countries of Western Europe, North America, Japan and Oceania, the national average of total government outlays (unweighted by population, but exclusive of Iceland and Luxembourg) in 1960 was 24.7 per cent of GDP. By 2005 it stood at 44 per cent. For the G7, public outlays increased from 28 per cent of their total combined GDP in 1960 to 44 per cent in 2005. True, the expenditure share in both cases was a couple of percentage points higher during the recession years of the early nineties than at the booming end of the decade, but that should be interpreted as a largely conjunctural oscillation. In terms of taxes, in 2006 the OECD beat its own historical record of tax revenue, from 2000, and registered its highest revenue ever, about 37 per cent of GDP flowing into public coffers. This is not to argue that there is not a growing need and demand for education, health and social services, and retirement income, which will require the further growth of the welfare state, a growth currently stultified by right-wing forces.

The second new state form – its breakthrough again coming in the sixties (following a pre-war take-off in Japan) – has been that of the East Asian outward-development model: oriented towards exports to the world market, biased towards heavy manufacturing, characterized by state planning and control of banks and credit, and indeed, sometimes, as in Korea, by full state ownership. Pioneered by Japan,

---

4. 1960 data from *OECD Historical Statistics 1960–1997*, Paris: OECD, 1999, tables 6.5, 6.12; 1999 data from *OECD Economic Outlook*, Paris: OECD, 2000, annex tables 28, 29.

the development state soon became – with varying combinations of state intervention and capitalist enterprise – a regional model, with South Korea (perhaps now the archetype), Taiwan, Singapore and Hong Kong blazing the trail for Thailand, Malaysia, Indonesia and, less successfully, the Philippines (the latter, culturally and socially, is something of a Latin America in Southeast Asia, with its powerful landowning oligarchy still in place, for instance). These were the examples that China would draw upon from the late seventies onward; as, a decade later, would Vietnam. There is considerable variation between these states and their differing forms of capitalism but all arose within a common regional context – a Cold War frontier receiving a great deal of US economic (and military) assistance. All shared several features: Japan as the regional development model, a broken, or absent, landed oligarchy; a high rate of literacy; a strong entrepreneurial stratum, usually diaspora Chinese. For the most part, they have also had similar political regimes: authoritarian yet strongly committed to national economic development through international competitiveness, with the will to implement decisive state initiatives.

This sixties legacy remains a major feature of the world today. China, the largest country on the planet, has become history's most successful development state, with a twenty-year growth rate per capita of almost 10 per cent per year. The crisis of 1997–98 hit Korea and Southeast Asia pretty hard but, with the possible exception of strife-torn Indonesia, it did not result in a lost decade. On the contrary, most countries – Korea above all – have already vigorously bounced back.

The Western European welfarist and East Asian development states were rooted in very differently patterned societies, and their political priorities have been quite distinct. But *qua* states, and economies, they have had two important features in common. Firstly, they are both outward looking, dependent on exports to the world market. Contrary to conventional opinion, there has been a significant, and consistent, positive correlation between world-market dependence and social-rights munificence among the rich OECD countries: the more dependent a country is on exports, the greater its social generosity.[5] Secondly, for all their competitive edge and receptivity to the new, neither the welfarist nor the development states are wide open to the winds of the world market. Both models have established, and continue to maintain, systems of domestic protection. Among the welfare states, this takes the form of social security and income redistribution. When Finland, for instance, was hit by recession in the early nineties, with a 10 per cent decline of GDP and unemployment climbing to nearly 20 per cent, the state stepped in to prevent any increase in poverty, thereby maintaining one of the most egalitarian income distributions in the world. While I am writing this, the Finnish economy is riding high again, and Finnish Nokia currently reigns as the world leader in mobile phones. By European standards, the Canadian welfare state is not particularly developed; nevertheless, despite Canada's close ties with its massive neighbour – reinforced through NAFTA – it has been able to maintain its more egalitarian income distribution over the past twenty years, whereas US inequality has risen sharply.

The Asian development states have been more concerned with political and cultural protection against unwanted foreign influences, often adopting an authoritarian nationalist stance. Japan and South Korea have waged low-key but tenacious and effective battles against incoming foreign investment. The IMF and, behind it, the US attempt to use the East Asian crisis of 1997–98

---

5. In the mid-nineties the Pearson correlation measure of exports and social expenditure as a percentage of GDP in the original OECD countries was 0.26. There is probably no direct cause and effect here. Rather, the link should be interpreted as meaning that international competitiveness has contributed, through growth, to the weight of progressive forces, and has not been incompatible with the latter's policies of extending social entitlements.

to force open the region's economies has met with only modest success; Malaysia even managed to get away with imposing a set of controls on transborder capital flows.

State Failures

On the other hand, there has been a lethal crisis among economically inward-looking, low-trade states. The shielded Communist models have imploded, with the exception of North Korea, which barely remains afloat. China, Vietnam, Cambodia and Laos have all staked out a new course: China now has a proportionately larger block of foreign investment than Latin America. Cuba has managed to survive despite the US blockade – even after the disappearance of the Soviet Union – largely through mutating into a tourist destination, with the help of capital from Italy, Canada and Spain (although that capital is currently being overtaken by Venezuelan money in return for Cuban educational and medical aid). In Africa, the postcolonial states with national 'socialist' ambitions have failed miserably, through a lack of both administrative and economic competence and a suitable national political culture. South Asia had better initial conditions, with a qualified administrative elite, a significant domestic bourgeoisie and a democratic culture. But the outcome has been disappointing, with an exclusionary education system and low economic growth leading to an increase in the numbers of people living in poverty. Even after India's recent moves onto a path of economic growth, it remains the largest poorhouse on earth. About 40 per cent of the world's poor (living on less than $2 a day) are in South Asia, 75–80 per cent of the regional population. The turn towards import-substituting industrialization in Latin America in the fifties was not without success, especially in Brazil. But it was clear by the seventies and eighties that the model had reached a dead end. By then, the entire region had run into a deep crisis, economic as well as political. Traditionalist, inward-oriented states such as Franco's Spain were also forced to change: beginning in about 1960, Spain took a new tack, concentrating on mass tourism and attracting foreign investment.

The widespread crises faced by this type of inward-looking state, in all its many incarnations – in sharp contrast to the successes of the different versions of the two outward-looking state forms – must have some general explanation. It should probably be sought along the following lines. The period after the Second World War saw a new upturn in international trade – although by the early seventies, it had only reached the same proportion of world trade as that of 1913. More important than its scale, however, was its changing character. As became clear by the end of the twentieth century, international trade has been decreasingly an exchange of raw materials against industrial commodities – predominant in the Latin American age of export orientation – and increasingly a competition among industrial enterprises. One effect of this growth of intra-industrial trade has been a great boost to technology; thus, countries standing aside from the world market have tended to miss out on this wave of development. By the early eighties, when the USSR finally managed to surpass the US in steel production, steel had become an expression of economic obsolescence rather than a signifier of industrial might. Somewhere between the enthusiasm over *Sputnik* (1957) and the pre-crisis stagnation of the 1980s, the Soviet Union – which had always borrowed its industrial goal-models from the West, from the US above all – slacked off in its technological dynamic. The Western post-industrial turn and the new possibilities of electronics were discovered too late by the Soviet and Eastern European planners.

A state, then, can still assert itself and implement its own policies under current conditions of globalization – provided that its economy can compete on the world market. To the classical Left, this is a new challenge, but it was something the Scandinavian labour movement grew up with, in small, little-developed societies that turned their attention to the production of competitive exports by relatively skilled labour.

Corporations and States

The relative economic importance of the largest corporations has grown over the long historical haul – creating a concentration of capital, just as Marx predicted. In 1905, the fifty largest US corporations, by nominal capitalization, had assets equal to 16 per cent of GNP. By 1999, the assets of the fifty largest US industrial companies amounted to 37 per cent of GNP. For the UK's ten largest industrial companies, the rise was from 5 per cent of GNP in 1905 to 41 per cent in 1999 – of which Vodafone, the world's largest mobile phone operator, had 18 per cent.[6] Compared with the growth of the state, however, corporate growth is not always so outstandingly impressive. Perhaps surprisingly, although the figures are not quite comparable, it seems that the US state has actually grown faster than industrial corporations during the course of the twentieth century (although in the UK, the reverse is true). Public expenditure in the US more than quadrupled between 1913 and 1998, rising from 7.5 to 33 per cent of GDP; in the UK it trebled, from 13 to 40 per cent.[7] In Sweden, too, the state has outgrown the corporations. The capital assets of the country's three largest industrial corporations amounted to 11–12 per cent of GNP in 1913 and 1929, went down to 5 per cent in 1948, and reached 28–29 per

---

6. The capital balance – in principle, a balance of assets versus shares and debt – of the historical record may not be quite the same as the current accounting of corporate assets, but that change in turn corresponds to actual corporate development. Calculations from P.L. Payne, 'The Emergence of the Large Scale Company in Great Britain', *Economic History Review* 20, 1967, 540–1, and British and US historical national accounts; compared with contemporary data from *Fortune*, 31 July 2000, and from the World Bank's *World Development Report* 2000/2001.
7. N. Crafts, 'Globalization and Growth in the Twentieth Century', in IMF, *World Economic Outlook, Supporting Studies*, Washington, DC: IMF, 2001, 35.

cent in 1999. Public taxes, on the other hand, rose from 8 per cent of GNP in 1913 to 52 per cent in 1997.

Over the more recent period, growth relations between transnational corporations and national economies have been surprisingly nuanced. The revenue – a measure not usually available for long-term comparisons – of the world's ten largest corporations has decreased, relative to the world's largest national economy. In 1980, their sales revenue amounted to 21 per cent of US GDP; in 2006, to only 17 per cent; in 1980, corporate revenue was three times the GDP of Mexico; in 2006, twice that of Mexico, whose population was then around 105 million. We are, nevertheless, facing big private forces. In 1999, the total revenue of the world's 500 largest corporations amounted to 43 per cent of the world product. Their annual profits alone were 29 per cent larger than the GNP of Mexico, whose 1999 population was around 97 million people.[8] It is the wealth rather than the revenue of corporations that has increased in relation to states and national economies. Contrary to current assumptions, corporate revenue has not quite kept up with the growth of core economies in the past two decades.[9]

Market Dynamics

Even more than corporations, it is markets – transnational markets – that have grown. The financing of the US war in Vietnam was probably one of the turning-points in the economic history of the twentieth century: it helped to spawn the new transnational currency market with its gigantic capital flows, and American war purchases played a crucial

---

8. Corporations data from *Fortune*, 24 July 2000. GDP data from *World Development Report* 2000/2001.

9. Corporate account assets are more stable than market capitalization – i.e., the stock-market value of the corporation's shares on a given day. On 24 April 2000, at the very start of the downturn on the world's stock exchanges, the market value of Microsoft was almost 7 per cent of US GDP in 1999, and that of General Electric almost 6 per cent; see the *Financial Times*, 4 May 2000.

role in the take-off of East Asian development. On a world scale, stock-market turnover increased from 28 per cent of the world product in 1990 to 81 per cent in 1998. US stock-market capitalization rose from about 40 per cent of GDP in 1980, to 53 per cent in 1990, to 150 per cent by early 2001, after peaking at around 180 per cent.[10] Transnational capital flows have speeded up to an enormous extent, not only – probably not even mainly – thanks to innovations in communications technology, but because of institutional change. Two examples come to mind, the first of which is the transnational currency market. The postwar trans-national anchorage of the currency system, set up at Bretton Woods, collapsed in the early seventies. Transnational currency trading soon became an enormous global casino, amounting to 12 times world exports in 1979 and 61 times world exports in 1989, and then levelling off on this *altiplano*. In April 1998 the daily turnover of foreign-currency trading in the world was 3.4 times larger than the Mexican GNI for the whole year. Since the autumn of 1998, however, with the introduction of the euro and the fallout from the Asian crisis, among other factors, currency trading has declined significantly. In April 2007 the daily turnover of foreign exchange markets was $3.2 trillion, more than the annual GDP of the world's third largest economy, Germany, with a GDP in 2006 of $2.9 trillion.

The second change has been the development of signif-icant new objects of trade. One such invention – contrived in the seventies, but exploding in the eighties – was that of derivatives: betting on the future. Between 1986 and 1996, derivatives trading multiplied fifty-six-fold, reaching a volume of around $34,000 billion. In 1995, the notional amount of bets outstanding in global derivatives trading almost equalled the whole world product; since 1996, they have surpassed it. Cross-border flows of bonds and equities rose in the eighties and soared to a peak in 1998. Trans-national transactions on bonds and equities that involved

---

10. The World Bank, *World Development Indicators*, Washington, DC: The World Bank, 2005, table 5.4.

US residents rose from 6.9 per cent of US GDP in 1975–9 to 221.8 per cent in 1998 – more than twice US GDP – before declining to 189 per cent in 1999.[11]

A hundred and fifty years ago, Marx foresaw a historical tendency of development – that the productive forces would acquire a more social character and would thus come into increasing contradiction with the private ownership of the means of production. From that period until about 1980, there was indeed a long-term trend towards the socialization and/or public regulation of the means of production, transport (railways, airlines, rapid transit) and communications (telephones and, later, broadcasting). This was a major dynamic in the capitalist heartlands from the First World War to the beginning of the Cold War. It was buttressed by the might of Soviet industrialization and, after the Second World War, by the entire Communist bloc. Still another socializing wave came with postcolonial socialism, the Cuban revolution, the Chilean Unidad Popular and the socialization proposals of the French and Swedish governments between the mid-seventies and the early eighties.

Then the trend reversed, with failures and defeats from Sweden to Chile, from France to Tanzania to India, accompanied by a mounting crisis in the Communist countries. In Britain the wave of privatization was initiated by Thatcher – in this respect, more radical than her Chilean counterpart, Pinochet. Since then, privatization programmes have been adopted not only in post-Communist Eastern Europe but also in the largest remaining Communist countries, China and Vietnam, and by virtually all social democracies – not to speak of the Right. Such programmes have become a major, sometimes a decisive, condition

---

11. The World Bank, *World Development Indicators*, Washington, DC: The World Bank, 2000, table 5.2; *Dagens Nyheter*, 12 April 2001, C3; David Held et al., *Global Transformations*, Stanford, CA: Stanford University Press, 1999, 208–9; Bank for International Settlements, *70th Annual Report*, Basle: Bank for International Settlements, 2000.

for IMF loans. How can this historical turn from socialization to privatization be explained? What happened
was a confluence of three systemic processes, under the
conditions – favourable or unfavourable, depending on one's
point of view – of contingent events.

1. The development programme of the Communist states,
dependent on mobilizing natural and human resources
with the help of existing technology, domestic or borrowed,
was beginning to exhaust itself. This first became visible
in East Central Europe by the mid-sixties and in the Soviet
Union about a decade later. Outside the domain of the
arms race with the US, the question of how to generate
new technology and more productivity was never
answered. The Soviet invasion of Czechoslovakia in 1968
froze new Communist initiatives and inaugurated a period
of stagnation, which *perestroika* could not disrupt.

2. The competence and integrity of the postcolonial states
turned out to be fatally inadequate to the requirements of
social planning and state-sponsored economic development.

3. In the core capitalist countries, new sources of capital
generation and management technologies challenged the
capacity of the state. Heavy social commitments also made
it increasingly difficult for even wealthy states to meet new
demands for investment in infrastructure, while the explosion
of financial markets generated much more private capital.

These three systemic tendencies coalesced in the
eighties. Privatization then gained its own political
thrust through the emergence of two particularly ruthless
and strong-willed tendencies, both arising out of the
Left's failed crisis management: *Pinochetismo* in Chile
and Thatcherism in Britain. In neither case was privatization
initially an issue – beyond undoing Allende's socializations
– but rather something which emerged, early on, from within

the leader's entourage. Once put on track, though, it was vigorously pushed by interested investment bankers and business consultants, turned into a condition of IMF–World Bank loans, and taken up as an ideological centrepiece by the right-wing media. As was noted, there have been some technological aspects to this shift, mainly in telecommunications, and some managerial aspects. Private-sector outsourcing has been a parallel development. But overall, the privatization drive has been powered by new private capital, strongly supported by ideological fashion.

Less Class, More Irreverence

Industrial employment peaked in the capitalist heartlands in the second half of the sixties; the industrial working-class movement reached the historical height of its size and influence in the seventies; and a fairly dramatic process of deindustrialization took place in the eighties.[12] While industrialization and industrial working-class formation continued in East and Southeast Asia, most powerfully in South Korea – where manufacturing employment soared from 1.5 per cent in 1960 to 22 per cent in 1980, peaking in 1990 at 27 per cent of total employment – deindustrialization also hit old Third World industrial centres, such as Bombay. Manufacturing employment also declined, relatively, beginning in 1980 in all the more developed Latin American countries (save Mexico, with its US-operated *maquiladoras*).[13] Between 1965 and 1990, industrial employment as a proportion of world employment declined from 19 to 17 per cent, and among the 'industrial countries' from 37 to 26 per cent.[14] A later ILO time series, 1996–2006, indicates a certain stabilization at a slightly higher level, with industrial

---

12. See my *European Modernity and Beyond*, London: Sage Publications, 1995, 69ff.

13. CEPAL, *Panorama social de América Latina, 1997*, Santiago de Chile: UN, 1997, table III.3.

14. ILO, *World Employment 1995*, Geneva: ILO, 1995, 29.

employment making up 21 per cent of world employment at both end years, in as much as post-industrial decline was offset by South Asian industrialization.

Clearly, however, the great epoch of the industrial working-class movement has come to an end. In fact, industrial labour came to dominate post-agrarian employment only in Europe, never in the US, Japan or South Korea, and it is most unlikely to happen ever again. Once more according to the ILO, service employment is on the verge of overtaking industrial employment in China. The enormous growth of Third World megacities – from Cairo to Jakarta, from Dhaka to Mexico via Kinshasa and Lagos – is generating an urban proletariat only in the Roman, pre-Marxist sense of 'informal' labour and dealers. In India, only about a tenth of the economically active population is in the formal urban sector; in China, 23 per cent. While an international slum-dwellers organization exists, an eventual revolt of the slums (as suggested in Mike Davis's *Planet of Slums*), if it occurs, is unlikely to fit into the classical repertoire of working-class protest and revolution. Classical 'irreverent collectivism', of which the industrial working-class movement was the main historical carrier, has passed its high point and is now progressively weakening. But this is only part of the story.

The other crucial development over this period has been the strong erosion of traditional deference, religious as well as sociopolitical. De-agrarianization has been one factor here – agricultural labour declining from 57 to 48 per cent of world employment between 1965 and 1990 – although peasants have been far from always and everywhere deferential. According to the 2000 census, town-dwellers in China now make up a good third of the population; ten years ago, they constituted a quarter. The Netherlands provides a stark example of secularization: the explicitly religious parties received over half of all votes cast in every election from the introduction of universal suffrage in 1918 up until 1963; their share then dropped to one-third in the twenty years that followed. The grip of patriarchy, too, has been significantly loosened: women's rights and questions of gender equality have appeared on the agenda virtually everywhere in the world.[15]

What we might call social modernization – resulting from economic change, education, mass communication, formal democratic rights, transnational migrations – has had the effect of eroding many different kinds of deference, affecting not only women and young people but also the salaried middle strata in most countries, the lower castes and 'untouchables' in South Asia, indigenous peoples on all continents, the urban poor in the new big-city slums of the Third World, Catholics and European Protestants. This developmental outcome was first visible in the sixties, with the undermining of traditional clientelism in Latin Europe and America. It was highlighted in the protests of 1968 and then by the women's movement that followed in their wake.

One element of this erosion of deference has been the creation of new forms of rebellious collectivism. Indigenous peoples have organized in defence of their rights and have become a significant political force throughout the Americas, from Arctic Canada to sub-Antarctic Chile, and a major force in Bolivia and Ecuador. In India, indigenous movements allied with environmentalist organizations have exerted veto power. Lower castes have reshaped their collective identity as Dalits, the downtrodden or oppressed, rather than polluted untouchables; women have worked to build transnational feminist networks. But there have been other trends as well. One is towards what we could call 'deferential individualism' – the worship of mammon and success in any form. The decline of erstwhile authority has also given rise to new, self-chosen brands of authoritarianism or to fundamentalism – particularly significant within American Protestantism, West Asian and

---

15. See Part 1 of my *Between Sex and Power, Family in the World 1900–2000*, London: Routledge, 2004.

North African Islam and Israeli Judaism. While Islamic fundamentalism and Latin American evangelicalism have thrived on the social failures of both the secularized Left and traditional religious institutions, fundamentalist currents within Judaism and US Protestantism seem rather to be driven by specific concerns of identity.

It is impossible, at this stage, to draw up a balance sheet of the combined effects of all these social processes, with their many contradictions, their exceptions, their unevenness. But my impression would be that the overall direction in which they have been – and will be – heading is not only away from traditional collectivism but also, and more insistently, towards a greater irreverence in the face of inequalities and privileges, particularly those of power and status. From a left-wing perspective, these processes offer not only the potential reinforcement of further allies in the stand against deference but also the challenge of an individualist or a new-collectivist questioning of the traditional collectivism of the Left and the anti-imperialist and labour movements. Most importantly, however, these developments do not simply provide additional resources for the Left. They raise new issues and generate new questions of priorities, alliances and compromises. At the very least, for instance, environmentalism and identity politics can clash head-on with the developmentalism and egalitarianism of the classical Left. Irreverence may also express itself in repulsive forms, such as xenophobic violence or crime.

DYNAMICS OF THE POLITICAL SPHERE

Within these coordinates, further dynamics are at work. The most immediate are those created by the historical outcome of previous political contests. Here we shall simply list what seem to have been the most significant defeats and victories, successes and failures, of the past forty years for both Right and Left, as well as noting what parameters have changed across the political field.

Left Successes

1. The discrediting of explicit racism and the fall of colonialism. Until the sixties, European colonial rule over other peoples was still widely held to be perfectly legitimate. Blacks in the US were still denied human and civil rights. The decolonization of Africa, the defeat of institutional racism in the US, the overthrow of apartheid in South Africa and the defeat of US imperialism in Cuba and Vietnam were resounding left-wing victories, which altered the political space of the world in important ways.

2. The postwar argument over the welfare state within the advanced capitalist countries – did the new prosperity mean that less social expenditure would be needed, or that social security and proper social services had now become affordable? – was resoundingly won by the (reformist) Left, especially in West Germany, Scandinavia and the Netherlands, and ratified by a series of important election results around 1960.

3. The worldwide student movement of 1968 was a major advance for the forces of irreverence across the world, for it attacked not only tradition and reaction but also the complacency of social liberalism, social democracy, Communism and national revolutions. It rejected the formula of economic growth and expanded mass education as an adequate fulfilment of the classical Left–Enlightenment demands for emancipation and equality, and set new agendas for human liberation and self-realization.

4. The new feminist movement questioned male radicals' leadership of movements for liberation and equality in which traditional gender roles remained unchanged. Overall, feminism has been a movement of the Left in the broadest sense, although more so in Western Europe and in the Third World – questioning the masculinist rule of capital

as well as of patriarchy – than in the US. In the past, women's voting patterns tended to be more right-wing than men's, in spite of the tendency of the early feminist movement to align with the Left. But in the course of the eighties and nineties this pattern changed, in the capitalist democracies, into a female voting preference for left-of-centre parties and candidates (very clearly marked in recent US presidential elections).

Left Failures and Defeats

1. An important turning-point was the failure of the Left to cope with the distributive conflicts that broke out during the economic crises of the seventies and eighties. Western European social democracy – above all, the British Labour Party – US liberalism, Latin American populism and the Chilean Left were confronted with such conflicts, which led to ever deeper crises of inflation, unemployment, economic ungovernability and decline. Their failures paved the way for a powerful right-wing backlash – violent in Latin America but within the bounds of formal democracy in North America and Western Europe. Thus ensued the moment of neoliberalism, which is with us still.

2. The *rendez-vous manqué* between the protesters of 1968 and the existing labour movements. After its first wave of individualist iconoclasm, the former turned to mimetic early Bolshevik romanticism and 'party-building'. Disillusionment there in turn generated a good deal of right-wing liberal renegadism, *nouveaux philosophes* and the ideological storm troopers of the Gulf and Kosovo wars, as well as the self-indulgent individualism of the Clinton kids. A good part of the irreverent individualism of 1968 has persisted, too – sometimes politically expressed, as in feminist and environmentalist movements and in human-rights activism. But because of that missed appointment, the potential for a historical renewal or refounding of the Left was lost.

3. The Right's capacity for violence – fatally underestimated by the Left – led to a number of bloody defeats: Indonesia in 1965, the Southern Cone of Latin America in the early seventies, a more protracted but proportionately even more murderous struggle in Central America.

4. The implosion of Communism in the 1990s was a negative turn on an epochal scale, for the non-Communist as well as the Communist Left: the possibility of achieving a viable noncapitalist society lost much of its credibility. The demise of Communism was neither a heroic defeat nor merely the result of an accelerating process of decay. It had, in fact, an ironic twist. In both the Soviet Union and China, the beginning of the end was a wave of radical and unexpected internal reforms; in both countries, the denouement came as the unintended result of the success of these reforms. In the Soviet Union, the reforms were largely political and democratizing; they threw the planned economy into chaos and, finally, benefited nationalist politicians. In China, they were largely economic, taking longer to tear socialist politics to pieces while profoundly corrupting the party-state. Eastern Europe overtook the USSR, breaking loose before the latter disintegrated, and Communist Southeast Asia followed China rather cautiously.

Two smaller Communist regimes, however, have so far maintained themselves, through very different survival strategies. Nationalist isolation has mutated North Korean Communism into a dynastic power, complete with ballistic missiles and mass poverty. Cuba has survived with the revolutionary integrity of its regime intact, although this is hardly less personality-driven and authoritarian than what preceded it. Its ingenious strategy has been to become, once again, a major international holiday resort. While tourism is certainly an industry of the future, it is less clear that the beach hotel can be a medium-term social model.[16]

---

16. Many – if not most – of the best Cuban hotels are public property, but they are usually managed by foreign-based capitalist enterprises.

5. A further difficulty for the Left: neoliberal economic policies did bring some material rewards and could not credibly be denounced as a complete failure for the Right. Neoliberal governments succeeded in curbing inflation, a major political asset in the nineties in Argentina, Bolivia, Brazil, Peru and elsewhere. The opening of world markets meant new opportunities for quite a number of people. Some privatization initiatives succeeded not only in providing more privileges for a few but also in encouraging investment and providing services: telecommunications is the outstanding example here.

6. Geopolitical events at the state level have weighed heavily on the Left–Right balance of world forces. A brief list must suffice as a reminder. The Sino-Soviet split, later reproduced in the Pol Pot–Vietnam conflict, divided and demoralized the Left and enormously strengthened the hand of the Right. State breakdowns in independent Africa, beginning in the Congo in the autumn of 1960, left little space for Left politics and policy on that continent – a restriction camouflaged for a while by the geopolitical alignment of some leaders with the USSR. The catastrophic defeat by Israel in the 1967 war discredited and demoralized the secularized Arab Left throughout the region and bred aggressive religious fundamentalisms among both Arabs and Jews.

In addition to these successes and failures, we must register the ways in which the parameters of the political field in general have shifted during this period. Again, there is space here only to note the effects of some of these dynamics on the balance of Right and Left. Firstly, there has been the rise of environmental politics, which surged in the wake of the mid-seventies oil crisis. While generally more critical of capital than of labour, these currents have also questioned the fundamentally developmentalist perspective of the industrial Left, and may prove more tolerant of unemployment and economic inequality than the traditional Left has been. Secondly, the politics of ethnic and sexual identity have become considerably more important in some parts of the world. Their relation to socio-economic issues is often ambiguous – critical of inequalities that affect their grouping or community, for instance, but not of those that affect others or of inequality in general.

Impact of Technologies

New developments in scientific knowledge and technology over the past forty years have also had an impact on political space. First, we should note the effects of technology in the acceleration of industrial productivity, resulting in relative deindustrialization and, with it, the disappearance of traditional working-class milieux. Television has furthered the creation of new, home-centred social relations and of a more image-focused politics. Further developments in telecommunications – satellite broadcasting, mobile phones, email and the Internet – have been double-edged, eroding both public-service communication and also public-order controls.[17] Finally, more than a century after Darwin, biology is once more emerging as a site for the expansion of knowledge and technology, and thereby also for cultural ideology. The political field of the future will surely contain a larger element of 'life politics' around issues such as health, the environment, coping with ageing, genetic engineering, ethical questions and quality of life.

CULTURES OF CRITIQUE

Critical thought depends on cultural soil to grow. In order to make sense, a critique must depart from certain

---

17. This loosening of public-order controls may be reversed in the near future: an interesting test will be how the police authorities deal with forthcoming EU, WTO or World Bank summits. The technology for global surveillance and espionage already exists in the US Echelon system.

assumptions or principles embodied in its subject. The Enlightenment and its subsequent traditions provided an ideal starting point for left-wing critical thought. Critical enquiry, unhampered by existing authorities and beliefs, was enshrined at the core of the Enlightenment itself – *Sapere aude!* (Dare to know!) Its universalistic principle of reason provided a tribunal for critical accusation, against ancestral wisdom and the self-proclaimed heirs of the Enlightenment.

European modernity developed, culturally and philosophically, out of the Enlightenment and, politically, out of the French Revolution. Its political culture focused on the confrontation of the people/nation against the prince, the monarchical entourage of aristocracy, and upper ranks of the clergy. Although the forces of the status quo had strong institutional and intellectual resources to draw upon, the culture of European modernity was a fertile breeding-ground for radical critical thought; post-1789 Europe became the world's primary arena for ideological confrontation. So what was actually happening to the rights of the people, to liberty, equality and fraternity under industrial capitalism and landowner politics? The concept of class was forged before Marx in the first breakthrough of European modernity, in reflections on the Industrial Revolution in Britain and on the French Revolution. The value assigned to 'progress' tended to undermine the basic assumptions of conservatism.

As I have argued more extensively in other contexts, the modern rupture with the past took different roads in different parts of the world – a European road, a road suited to the New World of settlers, a colonial road and the road of reactive modernization from above.

In the new settler worlds of the Americas after independence, modern thought became the conventional mainstream, fundamentally challenged only by Catholic clericalism in Colombia and some other parts of Latin America. The main question in the Americas was not,

'What are the rights of the people?' but rather, 'Who are the people?' Does 'the people' include indigenous inhabitants? Black people? Uncouth recent immigrants? In a rough summary of New World political culture, two things stand out. Liberalism – in the broad sense of the defence of liberty (private pursuits, private property, private beliefs) and a commitment to science and progress (to reason) – has had a much firmer intellectual hold than in Europe, usually, if not always, overshadowing socialist critiques. Secondly, because of the much less pronounced ideological divides in America, Marxist thought and politics have on occasion more easily melded with mainstream political currents, such as New Deal liberalism; Creole populism in Cuba, Guatemala and Argentina in the 1940s; or Chilean radicalism in the 1960s–70s.

The anticolonial modernism of the colonized – a perspective also adopted in Latin America by those who rejected settler Creolity – was highly conducive to radicalism. The colonized moderns – the generation of Nehru, Sukarno, Ho Chi Minh and Nkrumah – were probably the people experiencing the contradictions of liberal European modernity most acutely. On one hand, they had identified with the modern aggressor, the colonial power – learning its language, its culture, its political principles of nation/people, rights and self-determination. On the other, they experienced the denial of rights and self-determination to their own people, the haughty face and the iron fist of liberal imperialism. Socialist radicalism, both Communist and non-Communist, was a pervasive characteristic of post-Second World War anticolonial nationalism.

Reactive modernization from above, by contrast, left little space for radical thought. By definition, it meant an instrumentalization of nation, politics, science and progress, with a view to preserving a regime – real or imagined – under external imperialist threat. Since liberty, equality and fraternity were predefined in the mainstream as a means of strengthening the regime, their intrinsic social contradictions were kept out of sight or sidelined from the beginning. This did not, of course, prevent radical currents from making their way, alongside modern ideas in general, into Japan, Siam, Turkey and the uncolonized Arab world. There, however, they encountered a more barren soil, as well as repressive vigilance.

Modernism – with its commitment to reason, science, change, progress and the future – was not inherently left-wing. (Chapter 3 examines the different 'master narratives' of modernity and their relationship to Marxism.) In the latter part of the nineteenth century, traditionalist conservatism was increasingly supplemented, and in the Americas it was overtaken, by a right-wing modernism that extolled the overriding rights of the strongest and the fittest. This was social Darwinism and the new language of liberal imperialism, both important ingredients of twentieth-century Fascism. However, after Stalingrad and Auschwitz, this racist, imperialist and militaristic modernism was both defeated and utterly discredited. Non-militaristic laissez-faire social Darwinism, promulgated by Herbert Spencer among others and very influential in the US, had its thesis of the antagonism between industrialism and militarism disproved by the First World War, and its economic credentials destroyed by the Depression of the 1930s.

After the Second World War, modernism was overwhelmingly left-of-centre in all parts of the world, except, by and large, the countries involved in reactive modernization. Then, in about 1980, came the avalanche of postmodernism. The same period that saw the eclipse of political Marxism also witnessed the denial of modernity in the name of postmodernity, and the rise of postmodernism. The latter has at least two very different origins.[18] One is aesthetic: a mutation of the modernist succession of avant-gardes, most clearly developed in the field of architecture as a

---

18. See the unrivalled critical archaeology of Perry Anderson, *The Origins of Postmodernity*, London: Verso, 1998.

reaction against the austere high modernism of Mies van der Rohe and the International Style. The other source lies in social philosophy, a manifestation of ex-leftist exhaustion and disenchantment. The key figure here is the late French philosopher Jean-François Lyotard, a disillusioned former militant of the far-left grouplet *Socialisme ou Barbarie*.[19]

Why did postmodernism become such a formidable challenge? Why was postmodernity 'badly needed, intuitively longed for, and desperately sought', as an early devotee recently put it, with the benefit of a more sceptical hindsight?[20] The aesthetic attraction is easily understood as, above all, another manifestation of the relentless modernist drive for innovation; what influences its specific forms would be in opposition to its immediate predecessor/enemy, as well as the sociocultural context. But the question of the theoretical and political significance of postmodernism still remains. Here, Jeffrey Alexander captures one salient point when he concludes that 'postmodern theory . . . may be seen . . . as an attempt to redress the problem of meaning created by the experienced failure of "the sixties".'[21]

All this involved a remarkable conflation of brilliance and myopia. In the cultural sphere, important changes had clearly taken place between the work of, say, Mies van der Rohe and Robert Venturi, or Jackson Pollock and Andy Warhol – changes emerging in the 1960s, and setting a new aesthetic tone for the coming decades. Those developments warranted analyses of a new mode of cultural production, such as Fredric Jameson's *Postmodernism*.[22] But even the very best attempts at relating

19. J. F. Lyotard, *The Postmodern Condition: A Report on Knowledge*, trans. G. Bennington and B. Massumi, Minneapolis: University of Minnesota Press, 1984 (1979).
20. Z. Bauman and K. Tester, *Conversations with Zygmunt Bauman*, Cambridge: Polity, 2001, 71.
21. J. Alexander, 'Modern, Anti, Post, Neo', NLR 1: 210, March-April 1995, 82.
22. Fredric Jameson, *Postmodernism, Or, The Cultural Logic of Late Capitalism*, London: Verso, 1991.

cultural analysis to socio-economic change never fully succeeded in articulating the connections between the two. Jameson bases his account on Ernest Mandel's *Late Capitalism*, a picture of the postwar world economy originating in the 1960s, which largely focused on the state regulation of capital and its insuperable limits, so Jameson does not discuss the 'later' post-1975 capitalism or the surge of right-wing neoliberal modernism.[23] Despite his seminal contributions, postmodernism mutated into a set of cultural–political attacks on modernity and the modern – a malaise within scholarly analytics.[24] Outside the specific audiences of architecture and art, it largely addressed the Left and the ex-Left, including feminism, and paid scant attention to the simultaneous rise of right-wing modernism in the form of neoliberalism or assertive capitalism.[25]

Instead, postmodernism fed on the demoralization and uncertainty of the Left in the aftermath of late 1960s and early 1970s euphoria. Its critique of reason and rationality thrived on the 'machinery of images' of the television society, providing sustenance to academic 'cultural studies'.[26] There were, in addition, two further pillars of the new edifice of postmodernity. One was the social restructuring that followed from deindustrialization – an epochal social change. Another was the critique of modernist progress that arose from ecological concerns, which were intensified by the oil crises of the 1970s and early 1980s. Environ-

---

23. Ernest Mandel's *Late Capitalism* was published in English in 1975; its German edition appeared in 1972 from Suhrkamp. According to the author's preface, the main elements of the theory of late capitalism were conceived in 1963–67.
24. See also Linda Hutcheon, *The Politics of Postmodernism*, London: Routledge, 2002 (1989); and Pauline Marie Rosenau, *Post-Modernism and the Social Sciences*, Princeton, NJ: Princeton University Press, 1991.
25. Jameson himself scoffingly dismisses the doctrine's intellectual attractions: 'no one is going to persuade me that there is anything glamorous about the thought of a Milton Friedman, a Hayek or a Popper in the present day and age'; see Jameson, *A Singular Modernity*, London: Verso, 2002, 2–3.
26. Anderson, *The Origins of Postmodernity*, 88.

mentalism may have found it hard to flourish in the esoteric ambience of postmodernist philosophizing, but its adherents have proved receptive to postmodernism. Indeed, mass-market imagery, de-industrialization and ecological blowbacks provided a social echo chamber for the post-modernist discourse of (ex-)Left disorientation. Against this background, the modern – the target of postmodernism's attacks – has been defined in a number of ways. Jameson's *A Singular Modernity*, for example, while grimly noting recent 'regressions' from an earlier 'consensus' around 'full postmodernity', cites the asceticism of modernism, its phallocentrism and authoritarianism, the teleology of its aesthetic, its minimalism, its cult of genius and 'the non-pleasurable demands' it made on the audience or public.[27]

Although the intellectual wave of postmodernism has now subsided, the right-wing revival of modernity persists. The contamination of social Darwinism by Fascism is being pushed under the rug, while globalization is staged as the survival of the fittest alone, free from Spencerian pacifism and accompanied instead by a loud neo-imperial drumbeat. The 'modern' is becoming the property of liberal reaction. 'Modernizing' the labour market usually means more rights for capital and employers. 'Modernizing' social services usually means the privatization of and cuts to public services. 'Modernizing' the pension system generally means fewer rights for old people. Rarely does the term signal more rights for employees, the unemployed and pensioners, fewer rights for capital, or more public services. Were socialist modernism a species, it would be almost extinct.

Progressive academic culture has declined the world over, as postmodernism has turned into sociocultural studies, a tendency that is more closely connected to dark-ening political prospects *extra muros* than the kind of

---

27. Jameson, *A Singular Modernity*, 1. But were asceticism, phallocentrism and authoritarianism really more characteristic of, and more universal in, modern than pre-modern cultures and societies?

virulent internal anti-leftism found within French academia and certain post-Communist milieux. Japan's once strong university-based Marxist economics, which survived the great postwar boom, has faded; radical historiography in India seems to have lost its once impressive vibrancy; and the left-wing intellectual–political essay has gone out of fashion in Latin America. The public universities have lost many of their brightest students to right-wing private institutions. The continental European and Latin American mass Marxism of students and teaching assistants is gone. University students have not only been depoliticized, their movements have also diversified and now include street battalions supporting liberal-democratic, pro-American 'regime change' in Serbia, Georgia and Ukraine, as well as the anti-Chavista opposition in Venezuela.

Academia, think tanks and public research institutes, however, still support a wide range of Marxist and other left-wing thought. The politically more insulated Anglo-Saxon universities fare better in this regard than do the Latin American ones, which are always more susceptible to political developments and ambitions. Non-conformism remains well represented at Oxbridge and in the Ivy League, as well as at, for instance, top universities in São Paulo and Seoul. Part of their strength comes from a matured generation, with intellectually oriented student radicals of the late sixties and early seventies having attained senior professorships. But in the last five to ten years a new, though smaller, left-of-centre intellectual generation has been blossoming.

Institutional innovation has also taken place. One example is the revitalization of CLACSO (the Latin American Council of Social Sciences) under the leadership of Atilio Boron and, more recently, Emir Sader, aided by Swedish and other external public funding. CLACSO has become an important inspiration to and financier of progressive empirical research; its work includes the monitoring of protest movements in Latin America, which have been staging an increasing number of actions in the 2000s, and the promotion of South-South contacts.[28] Its weaker African equivalent, CODESRIA, based in Dakar, has recently been reinvigorated. In the current research arms of the UN, one also finds several products of an earlier progressive era, particularly from the Third World, doing excellent work while exercising diplomatic caution. Latin America has also been a major centre of thought and analysis of the cultures of globalization, as can be seen in the work of Octavio Ianni and Renato Ortiz in Brazil and of Néstor García Canclini in Mexico, for example.[29]

There has always existed a strong subaltern anti-modernism, to which the working-class history of E. P. Thompson in England and the multi-volume *Subaltern Studies* of Ranajit Guha and his associates in India gave eloquent expression, and of which James C. Scott has been a sympathetic theorist.[30] The Marxist labour movement could usually accommodate it through its socialist critique of industrial capitalism. But now that the Marxian dialectic has lost most of its force, it is necessary to take a systematic look, however brief, at the current political implications of antimodernism.

Here we are interested in movements critical of modernism that are not, however, right-wing defences of traditional privilege and power. There are several such movements, and they tend to cluster in two groups, one challenging the call for 'progress', 'development' and 'growth', and the other questioning mundane 'rationalism' and secularism.

---

28. See A. Borón and G. Lechini, eds, *Políticas y movimientos sociales en un mundo hegemónico*, Buenos Aires: CLACSO, 2007.
29. N. Garcia Canclini, *Culturas Híbridas*, Mexico: Editorial Paidós, 2002; O. Ianni, *A sociedade global*, Rio de Janeiro: Civilização Brasilera, 1992; R. Ortiz, *Mundializacao e cultura*, São Paulo: Brasiliense, 1994.
30. Scott's classic work was *Weapons of the Weak*, New Haven and London: Yale University Press, 1985; but his *oeuvre* also includes *Domination and the Arts of Resistance* and *Seeing like a State*.

Among the critiques of progress and development, there is one that has followed the Industrial Revolution into the postindustrial world: the defence of traditional livelihoods by artisans, peasants, small farmers, fishermen and tribal communities. That defence is easily supported by an anti-capitalist Left in opposition, and has been adopted by the current Social Forum movement: 'We do not want development. We just want to live', declared a front-stage banner at the World Social Forum in Mumbai in 2004. But when framed in strong, unqualified terms, it makes no sense to the masses of the world, who are struggling to get out of poverty. As a movement, antidevelopment frequently fragments into isolated minority battles with ineffectual and limited support.

The World Social Forums of the 2000s have given rise to similar antimodernist protest movements from different countries and continents, and have also given them platforms and a sympathetic hearing. But that has been possible because WSF is a forum, a meeting-place – by far the most exciting one in the last two decades – and not a movement or even a force of common action. The critical culture created at the forums has been that of resistance to neoliberal modernism. The global amplitude of the latter's offensive engendered a wide range of losers and critics, who were brought together with Latin flair in 2001 by a diverse coalition of Brazilian social movements and French academics and journalists grouped around *Le Monde Diplomatique*.[31] Significant organizational infrastructure has been provided by the Workers' Party (PT) governments in Porto Alegre and Rio Grande do Sul, by French and other Trotskyists in the alter-globalist movement ATTAC, and by the CPI(M) in Mumbai. But in their ideological ecumenism, lack of a single control centre and truly global character, the WSF does represent a novel phenomenon in the world history of the Left. On the other hand, a

31. B. Cassen, 'On the Attack', *New Left Review* 2: 19, Januray–February 2003.

stimulating cultural space is not in itself transformative action, which has led to tense debates within the broad International Council of the WSF.[32]

Another current, as old as modernism itself, is driven by a commitment to a natural or aesthetic lifestyle, originally conceived as a protest against massive ugly and unhealthy urbanization. In the 1960s, this became a significant urban movement, above all in Western Europe and North America, against the demolition of historic city centres to make room for motorways and commercial development. It scored several important victories in big cities such as Amsterdam, Paris and Washington DC, as well as in smaller places such as Lund, my old university town in Sweden. Since then it has spread to other parts of the world. The radical Left – and to a much lesser extent social democracy and its centre-left equivalents – usually played an active role in these urban movements, and broad, winning coalitions have often proved feasible. The political irony is that such coalitions have generally also included a strong right-wing component of cultural conservatives, so that the credit for success is legitimately claimable by both Right and Left. Nevertheless, the pollution and traffic congestion of Asian cities, and Third World cities in general, testify to the weakness of and the urgent need for critical urban movements.

In some parts of the rich world, most notably perhaps in California, a kind of postmodern middle-class culture has also developed, its origins traceable to the youth culture of '1968' – individualistic, irreverent, hedonistic but not necessarily consumerist, unattracted by capitalism's relentless drive to accumulate. Open to idealistic arguments as well as to ecological and aesthetic concerns, this is a milieu to which left-wing discourse can connect. The youngsters of the North who attend the World Social Forums often

---

32. Cf. B. de Sousa Santos (2007), 'The World Social Forum and the Global Left', http://focusweb.org/the-world-social-forum-and-the-globalleft.html?Itemid= 150; C. Whitaker, 'Crossroads do not always close roads', http://wsfic-strategies.blogspot.com/2007/08/chico-whitaker-crossroads-do-not-always.html

hail from here. Although its new 'spirit of capitalism' is hardly on the verge of transforming the ruthlessness of actual world capitalism, as some enthusiastic theorizing seems to imply (with some caveats), it does provide new possibilities for dialogue and debate with the Left – as did the old Enlightenment liberalism.[33]

The ecological critique of developmentalism connects rather easily with both livelihood defence and urban-community aestheticism, but as a major movement it is more recent, traceable to the early 1970s and the impact of the (recently updated) *Limits to Growth*. Its original neo-Malthusian thrust focused on the depletion of planetary resources, which has been replaced by an emphasis on environmental destruction, currently centreing on the effect of man-made climate change. But the engineers' modernism, which built the Soviet Union and is now building post-Mao China, is as deaf and blind to environmental externalities as was the capitalist modernism hailed in the *Communist Manifesto*. In this regard, it is noteworthy that the first oppositional movements in late Communist Eastern Europe were very often ecological movements.

Environmentalism and developmentalism have reached a modernist compromise, at least in principle, in the concept of *sustainable development*. To the extent that it is taken seriously, that concept provides an important basis for critiques of and interventions against unfettered capitalism. Indeed, socialism would have made much more sense in the twenty-first century if conceptions of sustainable development had been developed out of socialist theory, rather than growing into a belated ecological qualification of capitalism.

In the second cluster of challenges to modernism, the secular universalism of the European Enlightenment, along with its offshoots of settler liberalism, anticolonial nationalism and reactive developmentalism from above, has

33. Cf. L. Boltanski and E. Chiapello, *The New Spirit of Capitalism*, London: Verso, 2006; N. Thrift, *Knowing Capitalism*, London: Sage, 2005.

increasingly been challenged and undermined by ethnonationalism, ethnoreligious movements and by a resurgent religious universalism. In different ways, these new cultural tendencies – which make a mockery of modernity's self-confident secular evolutionism – severely restrict radical critical thought. Their unexpected emergence also calls for a reconsideration of some of the assumptions of European modernity.

Marx, Engels and later great Marxists have always been much more shrewd and circumspect than textbook summaries of historical materialism would suggest. While ethnicity, nations and national conflict have no place in the latter, the former always paid attention to their strategic importance, from Marx's hypothesis on a linkage of future revolutions in Ireland and Britain to Lenin's and the Comintern's focus on national liberation. On the other hand, ethnicity as such does not promote critical and radical thought. On the contrary, ethnic/national mobilizations tend to foster ethnic cultural closure. The leadership, which usually has had a transethnic enculturation, may link the national struggle to global anti-imperialism and to universalistic projects of social change, to socialism or to communism, but their national standing is not based on this. Positions of anti-imperialism and/or socialism may therefore, under changed geopolitical circumstances, become easily discarded postures. Ethiopia and Mugabe's Zimbabwe are gaudy illustrations; another is contemporary Iraqi Kurdistan, whose regional leading family, the Barzanis, once flew the banner of Marxism-Leninism.

Until certain Second World War rapprochements in the USSR and certain post-Second Vatican Council shifts in Western Europe and Latin America, Marxism had been firmly planted in the secularist, anticlerical and often atheistic strand of modernism. Where the subaltern populations have a strong religious commitment, as is the case in most of the Islamic world, this has been a major barrier between Marxism and the people. But even in Indonesia, where a more open Islamic culture did not prevent the emergence of a Marxist-led mass movement, the massacre of 1965 fed on whipped-up religious fervour.

The failures of secular anticolonial nationalisms spawned a strong religious comeback, thoroughly politicized in the Arab Islamic world and in majority Hindu India; mainly apolitical in Christian Africa, except in the apartheid South; politically active but internally divided in Latin America into currents of Christian democracy, liberation theology and US-exported Protestantism (either right-wing or politically acquiescent). This religious resurgence, which also includes a powerful fundamentalist Christian Right in the US and an international revival of militant Judaism, has significantly altered the cultural parameters of the Left.

Between middle- and upper-class fundamentalism – whether Christian, Jewish, Muslim, Hindu or Buddhist – and the Left there is no common language that could facilitate dialogue, as there is, deriving from the European Enlightenment, with middle- and even upper-class liberalism. With the religiosity of the popular classes, however, there might be.

Historically, achieving any common understanding or any form of cooperation between strongly religious subaltern communities on the one hand and the Marxist Left and the labour movement on the other has been extremely difficult and rare. The Christian social movements of late nineteenth- and early twentieth-century continental Europe were usually set up by local clergy worried about industrial secularization, of which the socialist labour movement was the most important representative. The cultural antagonism almost always overshadowed their common social issues, poverty and misery, with which the Christian social movements were increasingly confronted. In spite of mounting friction and occasional conflict, these religious movements loyally preserved their subordination to the church hierarchy and to the political leaders blessed by it. Until the religious trade unions secularized, as happened in Austria after the Second World War, and in the Netherlands and in France in the 1960s, when the chips were down, the Christian social movements sided with reactionary and anti-Left authoritarianism, in Austria in 1927–34, in the Netherlands in 1918 and 1954, in Germany in 1933.

In the last third of the twentieth century, however, there occurred a seismic shift in a part of Christianity. Mainstream Catholicism and Protestantism generally became socially progressive, and often also culturally and politically progressive. Advocates of Third World solidarity and aid, environmental activists, poverty-alleviation projects, harassed immigrants and even religious minorities and persecuted political radicals could count on substantial support from mainstream Protestantism as well as from the Catholic Church. The Jesuits, long demonized by secular liberals and left-wingers, provided courageous support to popular struggles and to human rights, above all in Central America. Many were martyred by the local representatives of Yankee America for it. Progressive Catholics constituted a major component in the formation of the most successful labour party in Latin American history, the PT, which lifted the metallurgical trade unionist Lula to the presidency of Brazil.

Can something similar happen in the non-Christian world? Sinhala Buddhism in Sri Lanka and Hindutva in India seem to be purely ethnoreligious political movements. The Buddhist monks of Burma/Myanmar may sustain a democratic movement, but almost nothing is known of their social agenda, if any – although the autumn 2007 protests started as a protest against price increases for fuel. In the Muslim world, by contrast, there are definitely strong social currents. Hamas in Palestine and Hizbollah in Lebanon already function as Islamic social movements, even while cornered by Israeli might that is backed by the entire North Atlantic Right. There were similar tendencies in Turkey, and still are, but the AKP

(Justice Development Party) in its mutation into a governing party seems to take European Christian democracy as a social model, that is, seeing and presenting itself as a centre-right party with social concerns. In Indonesia too, there is an Islamist political movement with a social perspective.

Social Islamism is likely to develop further, having an almost unlimited supply of social problems in Muslim countries to nourish it. But it occupies an unstable position on a wide spectrum from theocratic fundamentalism to a politically secularized Left, and thanks to heavy Saudi, US and Israeli investments in the form of money and military terror, the former is stronger and more attractive than the latter.

In sum, the cultural space of the Left has altered substantially in the past quarter century. On the whole that space has narrowed, but the new challenges to Enlightenment modernism indicate new tasks and possibilities for left-wing thought and practice, as well as a call for a self-critical appraisal of the inherent limitations and lacunae of left-wing modernism.

GEOPOLITICS AFTER THE SOVIET UNION

Political inspiration and demoralization are much influenced by state power and by the outcome of state conflicts. The Japanese victory over Russia in 1905, for instance, was a source of inspiration to anticolonial nationalists not only all over Asia but also in Egypt and Morocco. After the outcome of the Stalingrad battle, European opinion – from occupied France to neutral Sweden – tilted left. The Vietnam War, unlike the Korean War, unleashed tremendous political repercussions on social movements throughout the world.

The twenty-first century starts out with a quite new geopolitical configuration, radically different from that of the previous century. As it now stands, there are three major novelties. One is the absence of any state counterpart to the big capitalist power(s). The Soviet Union – whatever it was "really" – was always perceived, except for the four years of its anti-Fascist alliance, 1941–45, as the state power of anticapitalism, as a scandal and a provocation to all currents of the Right. As such, the USSR provided inspiration to many socialists and anti-imperialists, and to others at least a certain confidence that another kind of society than prevailing capitalism was possible. The Soviet Union also lent substantial material assistance to radical states, Communist organizations and left-wing refugees. With the implosion of the USSR and its European dependencies, no one is likely to take them up. And except for intraregional Latin American actors, all those roles and functions have been left vacant.

Secondly, there is a general feeling in the world – North and South, Right, Left and centre – that the end of North Atlantic world domination is approaching. Compared with the explosive economic growth of China and the new vigour of India, the European Union and the extension and Asian deployment of NATO are off-Broadway shows. A South led by China, India, Brazil and South Africa is replacing the Third World. What this tilt of the globe will mean is still uncertain. Left-of-centre political forces are better located in the South than in the US or in the NATO world generally. All four countries of the Big South even have Communist parties with governmental influence, ruling in China and playing minor parts in the governing coalitions of the other three countries. But the meaning of left-of-centre forces is very unclear in China, ambiguous in Brazil and South Africa, and clearly minoritarian in India. A weakening of US domination will, *ceteris paribus*, increase the prospects of peace and strengthen national sovereignty. The rest is still open to speculation, whether of hope or fear.

Third is the de-territorialized world war launched by George W. Bush, with great help from Osama bin Laden and cheered on by Zionist politicians and ideologues both inside and outside Israel. Proclaimed to be a war of annihilation with a time frame of at least a generation, it has created a global battlefield in which the Left, and indeed any movement possessing any human decency, has no stake whatsoever – except that no side should win, and that the sooner both sides are exhausted the better.

It has been an extraordinary war, fought by relatively small numbers, but with 'theatres', as the military jargon goes, stretched across several continents. On the one side, there are well-paid, high-tech mercenary armies whose commanders, private or public, are all funded by the taxpayers; on the other, there are unpaid, low-tech, religiously motivated fighters. Sustained by volunteers, paid or unpaid, neither side depends much on wide public support, although the political bosses of the mercenaries must ensure their own (re-)election. Both sides have taken warfare to new depths of cruelty. The weaker side has concentrated on the weakest element of their enemy – civilian populations – albeit on a much smaller scale compared to the British and American bombings of German and Japanese civilians during the Second World War. Yet the bombs, missiles and occupations of the stronger side have killed more civilians than the other side, showing how thin the civilized varnish of liberal democracies can be. The cruel attack of September 11 by a score of fanatics unleashed a fury of cosmic proportions. As a result, two countries on another continent have been devastated, and the destruction of a third country, Iran, has been overtly threatened. More remarkable, however, are the worldwide abductions; the official use of torture, both in-house and outsourced; the establishment of secret torture chambers and concentration camps; and the official rejection of the Geneva Convention relative to the treatment of prisoners of war and due process of law. This extraordinary violence has been defended and even condoned by majorities of the US Congress, by European social-democratic leaders of the UK and Germany, and by Scandinavian liberals spearheaded by the Danish government, which has participated in the wars in Afghanistan and Iraq.

That revolutions and civil wars involve abhorrent violence has become impossible for late-born sympathizers with revolutions – or with, for instance, Republican Spain – to ignore, and rightly so. But a critical scrutiny of modernity must also reveal the mechanisms that drive liberal democrats to the horrors of Dresden, Hiroshima, Bagram and Guantánamo. The scale of terror remains different, but Stalin's road from violent poverty in the Caucasus, Tsarist oppression and the life-or-death Russian Civil War (abetted from outside) to the Gulag is no more incomprehensible than the career of George W. Bush from inherited political wealth, Yale fraternities and Texas sweetheart business deals, through the small-scale though highly symbolic September 11 attack, and onward to Bagram, Abu Ghraib, Guantánamo and the devastation of whole countries just by the stroke of his pen. Killing from a desk is, of course, always easier.

Communists worldwide were blind to Soviet terror and famines, but why is the same blindness repeated in the current media-saturated liberal world concerning the four million dead in Russia in the 1990s resulting from the restoration of capitalism? The answer in both cases is the same: total commitment to a cause, whether Communism or capitalism, blinds one to the cost. A very large part of the Left has now learned that lesson, but hardly anybody of significance on the Right has. So far, we have seen a vengeful repetition of historical violence by the liberal right (in the European sense of 'liberal'), cheered on or at least defended by most left-of-centre liberals. Any historical lessons regarding the costs of blank cheques of political support have been postponed for an uncertain future. But the record is there. The starry-eyed defenders of the Yezhovschina of the 1930s have been succeeded by their equally starry-eyed fellow-travellers of the Yeltsinschina of the 1990s.

Globally, the disappearance of the Soviet Union and the Bush war against the world mean a geopolitical situation much more unfavourable to the Left, which will have to wait for the Southern tilt to become more pronounced. Regional developments, however, are more variable. In Latin America, the situation of the Left has been drastically ameliorated in the new century. The cautious weight of left-of-centre Brazil provides a certain balance to the US, which is mostly preoccupied elsewhere. The alliance of Chavista oil money and Cuban professionals (doctors, nurses, teachers, political cadres) is sustaining not only the revolutions of Cuba and Venezuela, but is also providing much-needed help to Evo Morales in Bolivia, to Rafael Correia in Ecuador and to the Sandinistas in Nicaragua, and is encouraging Left forces all over the hemisphere – and occasionally, as in Mexico, it is frightening the middle classes even more. Chavez's idea of a Bank of the South, endorsed in October 2007 by Joseph Stiglitz, Nobel laureate and former chief economist of the World Bank, might become as significant as the Persian Gulf capital which is already making the US Congress nervous.

Many Latin American Creole settler-states, many of which actively promoted their 'Whitening' by nineteenth-century immigration, are now facing new *indigenista* movements challenging the very foundations of the Creole state. This challenge has gone furthest in Bolivia, now living through a process of reconstitution that is driven by the presidency of Evo Morales. Ecuador is now entering a reconstitution phase, and indigenous claims are getting louder all over the Americas, although thus far they have been contained and divided in Mexico and Guatemala.

North America

As the world's only superpower, the US is the lender of last resort to all reactionary regimes of the current world order. Outside the corridors of power, there has always been a courageous current of US opposition to imperialism, and it broadened in the face of the Bush wars, although it remained much weaker than in Europe. Opposition to war made moderate, rather than overwhelming, headway in the Democratic primaries of 2008, although pushed by Barack Obama and John Edwards, and especially by Dennis Kucinich (the latter two of whom dropped out of the race early). As could be expected, the 1999 Seattle coalition of protectionist trade unions, anti-imperialists and alter-globalists has not been sustained. The US is also the homebase of a vicious Zionist lobby – with an important Christian fundamentalist wing – which occasional free speech defence may defy, but which has no serious political counterpart. A telling example of its virulent militancy was staged in October 2007, when David Horowitz launched 'Islamo-Fascism Awareness Week', including a campaign against 'Jimmy Carter's war against the Jews', presumably referring to Carter's travelogue through apartheid Palestine.

In spite of intrepid and undaunted journalists, maverick idealist congressmen, a vibrant academia which still includes a quite impressive amount of intellectual dissent and critique, and an admirable though powerless opposition, the US remains the solid citadel of ruthless world power, explicitly defiant of international law or concern for non-American lives. During the autumn of 2007, prospects for the 2008 presidential election indicated that the American voting population learned little from the Iraq War, with the Republican contenders competing in belligerence and the leading Democrat signaling her preparedness to follow the warpath into Iran. That the more belligerent Democrat lost to the one more willing to employ diplomacy may offer a modicum of encouragement, augmented by the Bush administration's decision to send a diplomat to sit in on talks in July 2008 between the EU and Iran, and to send several diplomats to Tehran later in the year.

American world influence is clearly weakening, but to extrapolate from this a 'terminal decline' of US power is, so far, mere speculation. For the foreseeable future, the US will remain not only the world's overwhelming military power, but also the world's richest large economy, with dynamic high-tech industries in electronics, telecommunications, aerospace and biotechnology, and with a popular culture of film, television and music of unrivalled worldwide attraction – serious competitors operating mainly in national or regional arenas.

Canada, a member of the G7, has been able to preserve a more egalitarian social model, in spite of NAFTA, belying the untimeliness of the 'crows' cries' about the erosion of the nation-state. In the run-up to the Iraq War, Canada was more resilient than most European states, although now it is taking an active part in the war in Afghanistan.

North America is the main destination of worldwide migration, and the main backdrop of the unfulfilled dreams of migrants from the South. Canada in general, and Canadian cities such as Toronto and Vancouver in particular, have become centres of multiculturalism. This also means that the political ambiguity of cosmopolitanism is visible most clearly in Canada, currently under a conservative, pro-US government.

Europe

Europe is going in the opposite direction from that of Latin America. Neither the social-democratic electoral tide of the late 1990s – when social-democratic parties governed or were in the government of fourteen out of the then fifteen EU member states – nor the Left social dynamic of the French and Dutch referenda of 2005 has been sustained. The French political system prevented a consolidation of France's finest hour, when the country stood up against the attack on Iraq; on the contrary, the current French government seems to have taken over Tony Blair's previous role in supporting American wars.

One might say that post-Communist Eastern Europe was bound to become pro-American and right-wing, but in fact, the political process there after 1989 turned out to be much more complex. One reason was that the restoration of capitalism was far from a general success. On the contrary, it resulted in a deep depression, massive impoverishment and unemployment, while simultaneously presenting new opportunities, particularly for the young and well educated. Another was the understandable incompetence of the new anti-Communist politicians, who had few chances to learn about government during Communist times. As a result, ex-Communist political leaders from Estonia to Albania staged successful comebacks, including, for instance, Alexander Kwasniewski beating the North Atlantic hero Lech Walesa in a presidential election. But the ex-Communists were all awestruck by Western power and Western money, and many were personally corrupt besides. None of them created a robust party of social justice, and the Western European leaders offered them no choice of a European security system independent from the US. In the end, they were sucked into the maelstrom of NATO – including contributing to the wars in Afghanistan and Iraq – together with some variety of neoliberalism.

Post-Communist Russian politics has been very manip-ulative. It has never allowed any proper democratization, as it has continuously been run by a tiny clique in the Kremlin that lived on Western advice and aid in the years of Yeltsin, drew on the old security apparatus, and thrived on high oil, gas and metals prices during the Putin years. Under Putin, Russia recovered as a nation-state and became able to pursue its own national interests, which are neither antagonistic to nor identical with those of America. Their relation to left-wing interests is also completely contingent, but Russia after Yeltsin has acted as a kind of brake, slow and ultimately inefficient, to American belligerence. Nationalism has trumped any social agenda. Russian nationalism was the card that Yeltsin and his managers used against Gorbachev, with whom a reformed Soviet Union would have been possible, shed of the now irretrievably nationalist incorporations of the Tsarist empire – the Baltics, the Transcaucasus, western Ukraine. When Yeltsin became a representative of the West, the Communist opposition became mainly nationalist, remaining so ever since and never spawning any serious social-democratic attempt even remotely corresponding to the utterly modest East-Central European ones. Anti-Chechen, 'anti-terrorist' nationalist machinations outmanoeuvred Putin's more socially anchored and politically much more meritorious rivals. With the help of the oil and gas revenue, Putin turned out to be more skilful and became more popular than most people had expected. Because of him, Russia is back as an independent geopolitical player, adding a certain amount of pluralism to the Big Games.

Africa

Africa was dragged into the Cold War with the murder of Patrice Lumumba, the first elected prime minister of the Congo, who was perceived to be 'anti-Western'. Occasionally the war became hot, as when apartheid South Africa invaded Angola to prevent a 'Marxist' government from coming into power and were driven out by airlifted Cuban troops. The Americans kept control of the Congo, but the Soviet Union drew much attention, leading to phony but indigenous 'Marxist-Leninist' regimes in several countries, from Ethiopia to Benin to Mozambique, all of which were toppled or had evaporated by the early nineties. The Chinese, who ran their own race in the last decades of the Cold War, are now back with a huge appetite for African raw materials. Whether their generous offers of aid – rebuilding the destroyed transport infrastructure of the Congo, for instance – will leave more enduring development traces than have previous projects, East and West, remains to be seen.

With the democratization of South Africa, Nigeria and several smaller countries, and the onset of cooperation among them, a certain political stability and dignity are emerging in Africa, currently supported by a return of overall economic growth. Prosperous, democratic and relatively well-managed South Africa is providing some continental – and progressive – leadership, noticeable even in parts of francophone Africa. But everything positive is still very fragile and patchy.

In the centre, Congo-Kinshasa is still a black hole, infested with violence, plunder and misery, and in the south there is the unresolved crisis of Zimbabwe. In the west, there are the simmering Muslim-Christian and ethnic conflicts in Nigeria, and the immense corruption and scam economy that persist under a thin gauze of chaotic elections. In the north, the conflicts and internal wars of Sudan have drawn American and Western European attention because they pit Arab Muslims against Black Christians. More ominously, both the north of Africa – south as well as north of the Sahara – and northeast Somalia are being drawn into the new American world war. AFRICOM, a new US military command structure, is being set up in Africa, and in a spiral of mutual encouragement, African Muslims are becoming attracted to violent Islamism.

Outside South Africa, Senegal and Morocco, there are currently hardly any explicitly left-wing political forces of any importance in Africa. The most important contingent, the Communist Party of South Africa – the only true CP ever constituted south of the Sahara – is a party of trade-union and other cadres and intellectuals, very dependent on its capacity to ride the rough waves of ANC populist nationalism. The intellectual centres of sub-Saharan Africa – the universities of Ghana in Legon, Ibadan in Nigeria, Makerere in Uganda; the famous Marxist centres of 'development studies' in Dar es Salaam and (for a brief time after Liberation) Maputo were virtually destroyed by the crises of the late seventies and the eighties. Legon and Makerere are now returning to intellectual life, and Dakar always remained an important outpost of research and reflection, to a large extent through the persistent efforts and commitment of Samir Amin. Apartheid South Africa, because of its resources and because of the complex crevices within its racist rule, provided a few very significant intellectual milieux of progressivism. The University of Fort Hare educated Blacks, including Black radicals; some anglophone universities, the Witwatersrand (Wits) in Johannesburg perhaps above all, harboured a courageous and vivid White radicalism. Democracy, however, has now sucked most of the bright intellectuals, Black and Coloured in particular, into politics.

West Asia

West Asia is a small part of the world. But it has a global significance out of all proportion to its territory and population, because of three things: oil, Israel and Mecca. American dependence on West Asian oil makes control of the region a vital American interest. Oil revenue has made possible the survival into the twenty-first century of archaic dynastic regimes more similar to Tudor England than to the Georgian England that young Americans rebelled against. If Saddam Hussein and the sheikh of Kuwait had gotten rich from rice exports rather than from petrol, it is unlikely that the sovereignty of the latter and the weapons of the former would have mattered much to the Bushes.

Israel is the last of the European settler-states, which started in modern times with the conquest and re-peopling of the Americas but which may also be seen as descending from the crusader states of the twelfth and thirteenth centuries. Its origins lie to a large extent in a socialist Zionism characterized by a strong universalistic idealism. But that idealism could not survive the geopolitical reality – that Palestine was not a 'land without people, for a people without land'. Palestine was populated, and the Zionist project could not but become occupation and ethnic cleansing, surviving in a hostile context only through armed force and through resources drawn from abroad: immigrants, money and weapons.

In itself the Palestine conflict is rather small and local, but it has been projected onto the world stage for two reasons: its proximity to the dominant Western oil supply and the resourceful Jewish diaspora. The latter has made the situation of the Zionist settlers a world issue, drawing strongly on Euro-American shame and guilt concerning the Holocaust. And for Germans and Americans, for instance, it is of course much more comfortable to let the Palestinians pay the Euro-American debt of guilt than to let the Zionists create their ethnic state in, say, Bavaria or New York.

The Jewish diaspora is always able to call on American might to protect Israel, but because of its oil interests, the US must also pay some positive attention to Israel's Arab neighbors. That imperative makes killing off or deporting all Palestinians from Palestine – a genocidal *Endlösung* of the 'Palestine question' advocated by at least one minor party in the governing Israeli coalition – politically impossible. The result is that in spite of a gradual increase of Israeli land, wealth and armed power, the conflict persists. The area is a perennial war zone. Founded in war, Israel then attacked its neighbors in 1956, 1967, 1982 (Lebanon), in 2000 (the helpless Gaza Strip), and 2006 (Hizbollah in Lebanon). Israel was attacked by Egypt in 1973. Now the Israelis are preparing, together with the Americans, for a new war – against Iran. The conflict is further exacerbated and amplified by the proximity of Palestine and oil to the holiest shrines and the spiritual centre of world Islam. The Zionist presence and the American guarding of the oil fields are seen as an affront to Islam.

The secular Arab Left was discredited by the crushing Israeli war against it in 1967. The Iranian Left was repressed by the Shah and then smashed during the second phase of the Islamic revolution. The Baathists killed off most of Iraq's Communists, and their Syrian comrades were able to survive only by supporting the Assad regime. The Turkish Left, always squeezed between the ever-vigilant military, urban nationalism and rural conservatism, has been eclipsed by the social wing of the Islamic movement; and Palestinian Marxism – the Popular Front (PFLP) and the Democratic Front for the Liberation of Palestine (DFLP), two main factions of the PLO, as well as the Communist party in Israel – has been similarly wiped out or marginalized. The outcome is that what there are of democratic and social forces in West Asia are mainly, if not exclusively, Islamic. But so too are monarchist reaction and theocratic repression.

The academic milieux of the region – home to some excellent Turkish and Israeli universities, relatively resource-ful American universities in Beirut and Cairo, and a number of much less well-endowed outfits – do include a few ongo-ing currents of radical thought. But on the whole, most of the region is a tragic zone of darkness, against which the hedonism of upper-class life in Beirut, Cairo and Tel Aviv appears obscene. Several small sheikhdoms in the Arabian Peninsula, on the other hand, have been giving the region a dose of positive significance. The TV station al-Jazeera is becoming a major world news medium, and the English-language Gulf press, run largely by Indian journalists, offers excellent Web-based financial news.

Because of the imbrication of aggressive Zionist settlers, big oil and the holy centres of Islam, West Asia emerged during the second half of the twentieth century as the major manufacturer of world trouble, for the Right as well as for the Left. Today, it is more bloody and messy than ever.

South Asia

Through its involvement in Afghanistan and its role in the 1980s and early 1990s as a conduit of Saudi money for Islamist anti-Communism in Afghanistan and Central Asia, Pakistan has been drawn into the turmoil of West

Asian Islamist militancy. After September 11, it was pressured into joining the anti-Islamist crusade of the Bush regime, thus ripping the officially Islamic but divided country further apart. Aside from that, the geopolitics of South Asia is still largely shadowed by the Indo-Pakistani conflict over Kashmir, a conflict of only local interest. Indian as well as Pakistani nuclear weapons, too, are of local concern and significance only.

Traditionally, in the post-Second World War era, Indian neutrality has been a force of Third World reason, as far as it has reached. To what extent it may stand up to recent American courtship, in the face of stiff Chinese economic competition, is still unresolved. But it is worth noting India's important role in the attempts to shape a collective geopolitical leadership of the South, first by bringing together Brazil and South Africa with India itself to create a democratic Southern tricontinental, and later by including China and launching the G-20/G-22 group within the WTO. India is now also being courted by ASEAN with the aim of forging a wider, horizontal Asian framework. Nevertheless, India has no world leader of Nehru's stature in sight.

In contrast to Bangladesh and Pakistan, India hosts important radical movements of universal significance, as demonstrated at the successful World Social Forum in Mumbai in 2004. The Communist Party of India (Marxist) – the CPI(M) – serves as part of the federal governmental coalition, within which it has at least some veto powers; in addition, it has for decades governed the large state of West Bengal. Indian academia, once a major world centre for Marxism, still seems to harbour a significant amount of radical thought, whereas much less of it survives in the locally politicized universities of Bangladesh and Pakistan. The Mumbai Economic and Political Weekly remains an enormously important fount of information and analysis, with no international equivalent in its progressive academic austerity.

Southeast Asia

This is the part of the world where most of the postwar battles for and against Communism were fought. Anti-Communism inflicted its most bloody and crushing victories in Malaya, Burma, the Philippines and Thailand, and in the massacre of unarmed civilian Communists in Indonesia in 1965. Communists won their most resounding victories in the region – those of the Vietnamese – against the French in 1954 and against the Americans in 1975. At present, there is a renewal of Communist insurgency in the Philippines.

No wonder that the states organization of the region, ASEAN, has a conservative tenor, although not reactionary interventionist like the European Holy Alliance. Originally ASEAN had an implicitly anti-(Communist)-Chinese orientation, which has now become untenable, given the surge of Chinese markets. As a consequence, ASEAN is now trying to recycle itself as an Asian pivot, seeking cooperation both with India and with the Northeast Three: China, Japan and South Korea.

While the region contains active and even militant forces of liberal democracy, primarily in the Philippines but also in Indonesia and Thailand, it is a region of victorious conservatism, with nominally Communist powers in Vietnam, Cambodia and Laos that are nonetheless fully absorbed by market developments. Singapore, under vigilant if not totalitarian conservative surveillance, is the intellectual centre of the region and is investing heavily in enhancing its position. For reasons not completely clear to me, the largest country in the area, Indonesia, is remarkably weak academically.

Northeast Asia

The geopolitical weight of this region is rapidly increasing. Internally, the balance of power is clearly turning from Japan to China. Regional interstices may allow minor players to develop, such as the 'Korean Wave' in popular culture, but the centre of gravity is China, which is overtaking the US as the main export market of Japan and Korea. This is a region still divided by historical resentment and distrust – between China and Japan, between Korea and Japan, and including the controversial status of Taiwan, de facto an independent state but de jure a 'province of China'.

Japan and South Korea have both generated militant trade unions and student movements, important though minoritarian. Taiwan has been a fortress of reaction, now undermined and eroded by localist and democratic Taiwanese-nationalist forces. China remains a Communist power, which means that a more socially concerned option is still possible, although the country has become one of the most income-unequal in Asia, much more so than India.

Northeast Asia is the crucial world arena of the coming decades. The path of Chinese development will be decisive – whether a continuously controlled, capitalist takeover or towards the institutionalization of socialist markets. There remains a critical Marxist legacy in Chinese research centres, intellectual circles in civil society and pockets of the vast party apparatus; in addition, there is a lot of local labour and rural civic protest. So far, however, these elements do not add up to a significant national political force. The opaque inner workings of the Communist Party remain the invisible key to the future of China.

Seen from a global perspective, the Chinese world-view is much more circumspect, delimited and peaceful than the American missionary universalism, with its constant urge to hammer home the correct American view. Chinese world domination would allow more breathing space than American domination, but it would not necessarily be progressive.

POLITICAL SPACES OF THE EARLY TWENTY-FIRST
CENTURY AND A PERSPECTIVE OF TRANS-SOCIALISM

The Left is on the defensive. But it has powerful lines of defence. Irreverence is dismantling traditions of deference, oases of critical culture persist across the globe, and the surge of belligerent Americanism is being balanced by the sociopolitically ambiguous economic tilt of the world to East Asia.

The socio-economic, the cultural, and the geopolitical spaces of the twenty-first century are radically different from those of the twentieth. While economic inequality is again increasing after its historical trough in the 1970s, class structure of social forces is eroding. Class is most unlikely ever to regain anywhere the importance it had in nineteenth- and twentieth-century Europe. On the other hand, as traditional kinds of deference have faltered and shrunk, a new field of irreverence, both individualist and collective, has been opening up, creating a new structural volatility of political commitments and alignments. Markets have regained the dynamics that operated in the rich nations before the First World War and now hold sway throughout most of the world, testifying to capitalism's reinforced vigour.

The changes in the socio-economic space hold profound implications for the Marxist social dialectic. The new market dynamics reverse the tendency towards an increasingly 'social character of the productive forces', coming into ever sharper conflict with the private capitalist relations of production and pointing to a socialist solution. This tendency predicted for capital did in fact occur during the first two-thirds of the twentieth century, underlying the collectivization – under many different political regimes – of urban mass transport, railways, water supplies, electricity grids, credit institutions, strategic branches of production and investments in science and technology. Market dynamics and new means of private capital accumulation have made the once-marginalized ultraliberal calls for unlimited private capitalism into a reality of massive privatization, North and South, East and West, by the centre-Left as well as by the Right.

The postindustrial turn reverses the second basic pillar of the Marxist dialectic: that the development of capitalism generates an ever larger, more concentrated and more unified working class. Dispersed service workers, 'informal' sweatshop toilers and hawkers of the Third World may be more rather than less exploited than industrial workers, but that is beside the point. The Marxist view of social transformation was not predicated on compassion for 'the wretched of the earth' but on the capacity of the exploited and the oppressed to emancipate themselves through class struggle. Current social tendencies make such struggle more difficult.

Contrary to many recent comments, the nation-state is the social dimension which has changed the least. More of them exist than ever, and the demand for new ones continues. Nation-states are also larger and more resourceful than ever, in terms of revenue and expenditure. Boundary surveillance and boundary penetration have both expanded, the former to unprecedented levels and the latter – in international migration – returning to the same scale as a hundred years ago. As was the case then, a small fraction of migrants turn militant and subversive, provoking large-scale xenophobic reactions in the countries of immigration. A hundred years ago, the 'terrorists' were Southern and Eastern European (and very often Jewish) anarchists, syndicalists and other labour militants.

Secularized Enlightenment modernism, of which the Marxist labour movement has been a major part and which has provided a congenial milieu for radical, iconoclastic art and critical social thought, has been seriously weakened. Its left and left-of-centre was particularly hard hit, by distributive conflicts in the Anglo-Saxon countries (epitomized in the British 'winter of discontent' of 1978–9), by the failures and defeats of nationalist developmentalism in the South, by the stagnation and implosion of ruling Communism, and by the fundamental questioning of modernism by non-right-wing constituencies, subaltern popular movements, environmentalists, and forays into postmodernism by important currents of the intellectual avant-garde. In the Left defensive, global neoliberal modernism has in the new millennium provided a target large enough to assemble wide networks of resistance, physically brought together by the World Social Forums. This is a new critical culture with an implicitly hegemonic antimodernist thrust, which, however, is unlikely to be sustainable, either against more robust religious and ethnic antimodernism or against persistent left-wing efforts to create another modern world. A perspective of 'sustainable development' by a different left-wing modernity is yet to be elaborated.

The geopolitical situation has changed fundamentally since the twentieth century, most importantly with the disappearance of the Soviet Union. For all the left-wing critiques of it, the USSR was a major pole of orientation of the left-of-centre world, not only to Communists, dissident or not, but also to Latin European socialists, Austro-Marxists, left-wing labour, militant trade unionists, and anti-imperialist nationalists across the three continents of the Third World.

The twentieth century was the last Eurocentric century. Even the globalized Cold War between the US and the USSR, neither of them fully European, had its centre in Europe, in the division of Berlin, and its end-game was played out in Eastern Europe. Twenty-first-century geopolitics is becoming more open and de-centred with American military superpower diverging increasingly from new economic developments, in Asia and elsewhere, and by new networks of states. The ascendancy of non-state violence, enacted by mercenary corporations and militant volunteers, adds to the de-centreing of current geopolitics – although most of this violence is inscribed within the American imperial configuration, as either a defense of or an attack on it. However, the predominant actors in geopolitics are still nation-states, not global movements. While alter-globalists are protesting, the WTO, the World Bank and the IMF continue on their path. The peace movement may have mobilized the people and persuaded majorities in many countries, but wars came, still continue, and are still being planned.

Nevertheless, popular protests are neither meaningless nor powerless, even in geopolitical contexts. They clarify the ethical issues, and can shift balances of power and force choices among policy options. As a global ideology, neoliberalism has been both largely discredited and effectively pushed back, if not decisively beaten. In the opinion of a majority of the British public, Tony Blair, for all his rhetorical and other gifts, has been irremediably soiled by the dirty war on Iraq. The Vietnam War was decided on the battlefield, but the option to bomb the Vietnamese 'back to the Stone Age' became politically impossible because of the antiwar movement.

All these changes have profound consequences and implications for left-wing politics. For the time being, their general trend is to intensify the struggles for peace, emancipation and social justice. But that may very well change. Much more certain is that the new parameters require much fundamental rethinking on the Left. The new capitalist vigour, and the situation of less class and more irreverence, calls for something that goes beyond attention to 'new social movements'. Novel conceptions of societal transformation are needed. Enlightenment modernism remains an honourable tradition from a perspective of human emancipation, quite worth developing as well as defending. But its antimonies were too easily covered by the anticapitalist class dialectic, and its relations to non-modernist subaltern resistance and to ecology must be reconsidered. Via Lenin and Leninism, Marxism became a global ideological current. But Marxism-Leninism turned out to be an unsustainable modernism. In a post-

Eurocentric world, admirers of Marx have to admit this and adjust their positions, taking into account that with its secularized class focus, Marxism was a profoundly European movement.

This is the time to begin thinking, from a *trans-socialist* perspective, of a world beyond capitalism and its global joint ventures of luxuriant wealth and misery. Trans-socialism is a perspective of social transformation going beyond the strategies and historical institutions of socialism, the centrality of the working-class and the agency of the labour movement, of public ownership and large-scale collective planning of production. It is not 'postsocialist', because it does not imply an acceptance of capitalism as the only possible game and because it implies a rejection neither of the goals of historical socialism nor of the attempts to 'build' it. On the contrary, it starts from an acceptance of the historical legitimacy of the vast socialist movement and its heroic epic of creativity and enthusiasm, of endurance and struggle, of beautiful dreams and hopes as well as of blunders, failures and disillusions – in short, of defeats as well as victories. It retains the fundamental Marxian idea that human emancipation from exploitation, oppression, discrimination and the inevitable linkage between privilege and misery can come only from struggle by the exploited and disadvantaged themselves. It then continues by recognizing that the twenty-first century is beginning to look very different from the twentieth – not more equal and just, but with new constellations of power and new possibilities of resistance.

What might be the basis of such a trans-socialist political perspective? There are four dimensions that seem worth keeping in mind.

First, there is the *social dialectic of capitalism*, which continues to exist. How the congruity or incongruity of capitalist relations of production and the forces of production will turn out by the end of this century is impossible to tell. But the dialectic of class conflict still operates,

although not necessarily with system-transcendent implications. The spread and growth of capitalism continues
to strengthen the working class, other things being equal.
Workers' strikes and other protests are increasing today
in China and Eastern Europe, as they did yesterday in
South Africa and Korea and as they are likely to do in
Vietnam tomorrow. The very success of capitalism still
generates protest against its manifestations. Strikes and
rebellions do produce better wages and conditions, even
for the tightly controlled immigrant workers of the Arab
Gulf. A similar feminist dialectic is spawned by the expansion of women's education, which is likely to seriously
undermine the obdurate patriarchy of West Asia and North
Africa. For the foreseeable future, however, it is unlikely
that this class and gender dialectic in Africa, Asia, Eastern
Europe and Latin America will carry the working class or
women even to the levels they reached in Western Europe
in the 1970s and the 1980s, respectively.

Second, there is also a *dialectic of ethnic collective
identity* among oppressed or discriminated ethnic groups.
The breakdown of well-arranged hierarchies in capitalist
crises, as well as the availability of new means of communication to the disadvantaged – such as the 'scheduled castes'
becoming a factor in urbanized electoral politics in India;
the experience of Bolivian mine workers being a model for
the struggles of Bolivian *cocaleros*; the spread of the Internet;
indigenous peoples of the Americas and of South Asia gain-
ing considerable access to NGO financial resources – have
promoted the rise of vigorous ethnic movements.

Third, of increasing importance is a dimension classically
denied significance by Marxism, *moral discourse*. De facto,
it was always there in the working-class movement,
concerned not only with a 'fair wage for a fair day's work',
but also with 'human dignity'. For all its hypocritical abuse
by Anglo-American politicians, the global spread of human
rights discourse beginning in the mid-1970s opens up an
area of broad concern and possible argumentation.

Two aspects of this moral discourse currently stand out as urgent. One is a social anchoring or embedding of human rights in a conception of social rights, of life-course choice and life-course development. This necessitates the freeing of human rights from its overpoliticized Anglo-American construction which, for instance, treats the continued assassinations of trade unionists, human-rights lawyers, journalists and activists – in Mexico, Colombia, Brazil and elsewhere – as peccadilloes, but regards the imprisonment of political dissidents in Cuba as a heinous crime – while not simply turning the Washington–London consensus upside down. A consistent human-rights discourse means, more than anything, that all human beings have a right to grow, to develop, to choose how to lead their lives. This version of human rights has a venerable pedigree in labour movements and the Left: solidarity with all struggles against the denial of human social rights.

The second aspect of a moral discourse is *antiviolence*, which may be seen as derivative of human rights. Violence is a denial of human rights. The Bush–Cheney regime, applauded by Blairism, has shown how thin the veneer of bourgeois civility is, how easily it turns into terror-bombing, abductions, torture and killing. But Bush, Cheney and Blair are only gloating over a seismic shift of bourgeois and 'middle-of-the-road' opinion. The leaders of the German Greens supported the 'humanitarian' bombing of Serbia; German and Dutch as well as Anglo-American generals produced in the autumn of 2007 a new NATO strategy for nuclear war – 'pre-emptive nuclear attacks' – which may be translated into a new NATO slogan, 'Let us create two, three, a hundred Hiroshimas!' The peaceful Danes of modern history are now making war against uppity natives in both Iraq and Afghanistan while humiliating their tiny Muslim minority at home, actions electorally endorsed in the name of liberalism. The US Republican presidential nominee in 2008 sang 'Bomb, bomb, bomb Iran' at electoral rallies, while Hillary Clinton, one of the Democratic favourites in the primaries, threatened Iran with 'total obliteration'. Alongside the ruthless, albeit small-scale, terrorism of Al-Qaeda and other footloose militants, these manifestations indicate that violence has unexpectedly become the signature of the post–Cold War period of the early twenty-first century. A crucial line of moral demarcation has emerged between the bombers on one side – the rich terror- and missile-bombers; the poor suicide bombers; the humanitarian, democratic bombers; the Islamist bombers – and the anti-bombing, anti-occupation, antiviolence people on the other.

As recent developments show, there is no moral evolution – indeed, currently there is a large-scale liberal regression going on – and there has never been a moral dialectic. It could be argued, however, that there is now a wider field of moral argument, one that may hold a greater potential for transcending class and national boundaries. What will happen in this area is of mounting significance.

Finally, and fourthly, on top of a (most likely) truncated social dialectic and an enlarged but highly contested arena of moral discourse, the twenty-first-century Left has to tap into a third root: a commitment to *universal pleasure*. The meaning of Marxian Communism was human enjoyment, phrased in terms of a nineteenth-century bucolic ideal. The austerity of the revolutionary struggle substituted a revolutionary heroism for Marxian hedonism, and the latter did not appeal to the 'respectable workers' of social democracy. But after May 1968, the hedonistic, the *ludic*, the playful orientation of the Marxian original must reaffirm its importance. On the one hand, it is a question of the right to pleasure – universal rather than segregated – and, on the other, it is a condition of adequate institutions making opportunities accessible. Left-wing commitment to labour, to socially meaningful human rights, to anti-violence, should also envisage a universal society of fun and enjoyment. Only right-wing perverts have fun at the expense of others. Sensual festivity has been one of the crucial Brazilian contributions to the World Social Forums and to the possibility of another world.

2

Twentieth-Century Marxism and the Dialectics of Modernity

Students of parliamentary history are familiar with the idea of 'Her Majesty's Loyal Opposition'. Marxism, as a social-historical phenomenon, has been Her Modern Majesty's Loyal Opposition to modernity – always critical of and fighting against her predominant regimes, but never questioning the legitimate majesty of modernity and, when needed, explicitly defending it. Like many oppositions, Marxism has also had its stints in power, but its spells in government have been short-lived in their attractiveness and creativity, rather prone to produce doubt and disillusion, and only through the exercise of the pragmatics of power have they persisted.

Marxism is nevertheless the major manifestation of the dialectics of modernity, in a sociological as well as theoretical sense. As a social force, Marxism was a legitimate offspring of modern capitalism and Enlightenment culture. For good or bad, right or wrong, Marxist parties, movements and intellectual currents became, for at least the hundred years from the late nineteenth to the late twentieth century, the most important means to embrace the contradictory nature of modernity. Marxism simultaneously affirmed the positive, progressive features of capitalism, industrialization, urbanization and mass literacy, of looking to the future instead of the past and of keeping one's eyes fixed on the ground of the present, and, on the other hand, denounced the exploitation, the human alienation, the commodification and instrumentalization of the social, the false ideology and the imperialism inherent in the modernization process.

Liberalism and Enlightenment rationalism, including, more recently, post-Marxist social democracy and post-traditional conservatism, have represented the affirmation of modernity and have raised no questions regarding science, accumulation, growth or development. Traditional conservatism, religious or secular, girded itself against the negativity of modernity. The Nietzschean intellectual tradition, from Nietzsche himself to Michel Foucault, has sniped continually at modernity, Christian and – to a much lesser extent – Islamic democracy, Fascism, and Third World populism. Marxists were, on the whole, alone in both hailing modernity – and its breaking of the carapace of 'rural idiocy' and airing of the fumes of 'the opium of the people' – and in attacking it. Marxism defended modernity with a view to creating another, more fully developed modernity.

Marxism was the theory of this dialectic of modernity as well as its practice. Its theory centred on the rise of capitalism as a progressive stage of historical development and on its 'contradictions': its class exploitation, crisis tendencies and generation of class conflict. Once its main lines had been drawn in bold strokes in *The Communist Manifesto*, the Marxian dialectical method also paid attention to the gender and national dimensions of modern emancipation. 'The first class antagonism', Friedrich Engels wrote in his *Origin of the Family, Private Property, and the State*, is that between man and woman, 'the first class subjection' that of women by men.[1] One of the most widely

---

1. F. Engels, *Die Ursprung der Familie, des Privateigentums and des Staats* (1884), in *Marx-Engels Werke*, vol. 21, Berlin: Dietz Verlag, 1972, 69.

diffused books of the early Marxist labour movement was August Bebel's *Woman and Socialism* (1883).[2]

THE CONCEPT OF MODERNITY IN MARX

As passionate political analysts, Marx and Engels closely followed the national politics of their time, although most of their writings about it were responses to particular circumstances. From the late 1860s onwards, however, they did focus on a problem with far-reaching implications: how one nation's oppression of another affected the class conflict in each. The concrete case was England, the most advanced capitalist country, where, Marx and Engels concluded, social revolution was impossible without a preceding national revolution in Ireland. Marxists of the multinational Austro-Hungarian and Russian empires soon had to pay more systematic theoretical attention to the concept of nation and its relation to class. The major theoretical work to emerge from this effort was Otto Bauer's *The Nationalities Question and Social Democracy* (1907). But the strategic vision and the political practice connecting Marxism and capital–labour conflict with anticolonial and other struggles for national self-determination were first fully developed by Vladimir Lenin, in a series of articles written just before the First World War and then consolidated in his wartime study *Imperialism* (1916).[3]

---

2. Bebel was, of course, the leader of the foremost Marxist party, the German Social Democrats. The early Marxist labour movement, particularly in Central and Eastern Europe, involved a unique (for the era) number of women in prominent positions: Angelica Balabanoff, Kata Dalström, Alexandra Kollontai, Anna Kuliscioff, Rosa Luxemburg, Henriette Roland-Holst, Vera Zasulich, Clara Zetkin and a few others. Marxist social democracy was also the first male political movement to campaign for women's right to vote.

3. An excellent overview of the issues involved, as well as a concentrated selection of texts, is G. Haupt, M. Lowy and C. Weill, eds, *Les marxistes et la question nationale, 1848–1914*, Paris: François Maspero, 1974.

To see Marx and Engels as dialecticians of modernity is a late-twentieth-century reading, an expression of a period in which critical social theory is asserting its relative autonomy from economics and in which, above all, the very value of modernity itself is being questioned from a perspective of post- rather than pre-modernity. However, it should be emphasized that although such readings, pioneered by Berman, are new, they are not arbitrarily imposed.[4] While never theorized or admitted into the classical Marxist canon, a conception of modernity pervaded Marx's thought. In the first eight pages of the *Werke* edition of *The Communist Manifesto*, we learn about 'modern industry' (three times), 'modern bourgeois society' (twice), the 'modern bourgeoisie' (twice), 'modern workers' (twice), and once each about 'modern state power', 'modern productive forces' and 'modern relations of production'.[5] And Marx's 'ultimate purpose' in *Capital*, as he put it in his preface to the first edition, was to 'disclose the economic law of motion of modern society'.

Keeping hold of the two horns of modernity, the emancipatory and the exploitative, has been an intrinsically delicate task, more easily assumed by intellectuals than by practical politicians. The Marxist tradition has therefore tended to drift from one characterization to another in its practice of the dialectics of modernity. In the Second International (1889–1914) and in the later social-democratic tradition, the negative aspect increasingly tended to be overshadowed by an evolutionary conception of growing countervailing powers, of trade unions and working-class parties. The Comintern or Third International (1919–43) and the subsequent Communist tradition, by contrast, focused on the negative and its peripeteia by denouncing

---

4. M. Berman, *All That Is Solid Melts Into Air*, London: Verso, 1983.
5. K. Marx and F. Engels, *Manifest der kommunistischen Partei* (1848), in *Marx-Engels Werke*, vol. 4, Berlin: Dietz Verlag, 1972, 462–9.

the increasing evils of capitalism and holding out the hope for a sudden revolutionary reversal.

The purely intellectual current of critical theory or, as it was also called, the Frankfurt School, emphasized the contradictoriness and negativity of modernity without issuing any cheques for a better future. The classical work of this kind of thought is Max Horkheimer and Theodor W. Adorno's *Dialectic of Enlightenment*, written during the Second World War by two German Jews in American exile. While underlining that 'social freedom is inseparable from enlightened thought', the theme of the book is the 'self-destruction of the Enlightenment'.[6] The latter's calculating cunning is elaborated in the Homeric myth of Ulysses; its emancipated morality is expressed in the sado-masochistic fantasies of de Sade, its enlightenment of the people in the 'mass deception' of the 'culture industry'. To them, the anti-Semites were 'Liberals who wanted to assert their anti-liberal opinion'.[7] The 'ticket-thinking' of the American electoral system was in itself, in its reduction of individual differences, anti-Semitic.[8]

The Marxist dialectics of modernity thus flickered between the shadows cast by the death factories of Auschwitz and the shafts of light cast by the growth and organization of the working class.

MOMENTS OF THE CRITICAL TRADITION

Critique and criticism emerged as major intellectual endeavours in Europe in the seventeenth century, focusing on the philological scrutiny of ancient texts, including sacred texts.[9] In the next century, the range broadened

---

6. Max Horkheimer and Theodor W. Adorno, *Dialectic of Enlightenment*, trans. John Cumming, New York: Continuum, 1997 (1947), xiii.
7. Ibid., 200.
8. Ibid., 206.
9. R. Koselleck, *Kritik und Krise*, Frankfurt: 1992 (1959), 87ff.

into critiques of politics, religion and reason. In Germany in the 1840s, criticism enjoyed further expansion, after decades of postrevolutionary reaction, in the form of philosophical critiques of religion and politics. Engels and Marx began their lifelong collaboration by writing a satire of the Left Hegelian 'critical critique' of Bruno Bauer and others, *The Holy Family*, in 1844.

Nevertheless, the critical German theoretical tradition, which, taken broadly, included both Kant and the Left Hegelians, was carried over into Marxism. After all, Marx and Engels proclaimed themselves the heirs of German philosophy, and Marx's major work was subtitled 'Critique of Political Economy'. In German or German-inspired literature, 'the critique of political economy' long remained a synonym for Marxism.

The 'science' to which Marx was committed thus included 'critique' as a core element, and this critique was meant to be scientific. While Marx and Engels saw no tension between science and critique, the Western, mainly anglophone, post-1968 academic reception of Marx drew a distinction between 'critical' and 'scientific' Marxism.[10] Leaving aside the lineage and the merit of such a distinction, Gouldner's ideal types clearly conveyed a divide of cognitive styles and strategies in *marxisant* academia at that time. Yet this account gave 'critique' a narrower meaning than it had had before. Gouldner's 'two Marxisms' constitute a moment of the critical tradition, rather than the tradition itself.[11]

The twentieth century has hardly lived up to the standards set by Immanuel Kant and many others for the century of Enlightenment, namely 'the true [*eigentliche*] era of critique'. Rather, the place of critique in contemporary social theory is better understood with reference to the

---

10. A. Gouldner, *The Two Marxisms*, London: Palgrave Macmillan 1980.
11. A recent, more faithful elaboration of Marx's critique may be found in R. Meister, *Political Identity: Thinking Through Marx*, Oxford: Blackwell, 1990.

original location and authors of critical theory: a tiny group of brilliant German-Jewish exiles living in New York in the late 1930s.

THE GROUND OF CRITICAL THEORY

As a concept, critical theory was launched in 1937 by Max Horkheimer, director of the exiled Frankfurt Institute for Social Research, who was writing in New York for the Institute's Paris-published, German-language journal. He was assisted by his associate Herbert Marcuse.[12] The meaning of the term 'critical theory' was a philosophically self-conscious, reflexive conception of 'the dialectical critique of political economy'.[13] A key notion of the Horkheimer circle, later known as the Frankfurt School, 'critical theory' replaced 'materialism'. Horkheimer's closest intellectual associate, Theodor W. Adorno, wrote much later that the change of expression was not intended to 'make materialism acceptable but to use it to make men theoretically conscious of what it is that distinguishes materialism'.[14] That is indeed probable, because Horkheimer's position towards the real bourgeois world was rather more intransigent in 1937 than it had been in 1932, when he had first become the Institute's director and editor.

On the other hand, Horkheimer was always a skilled and cautious operator. From the start, critical theory was more a code for, than a criticism of, 'dialectical materialism'. As such, it had a special, although not unproblematic,

---

12. H. Marcuse, 'Philosophie und kritische Theorie' (1937), in *Kultur und Gesellschaft*, vol. 1, Frankfurt 1965.
13. M. Horkheimer, 'Traditionelle und kritische Theorie' (1937), in Max Horkheimer, *Gesammelte Schriften*, vol. 4, A. Schmidt and G. Schmidt Noerr, eds, Frankfurt: Fischer, 1988, 180. See also *Critical Theory: Selected Essays*, trans. M. J. O'Connell, New York: Herder and Herder 1972.
14. T. Adorno, *Negative Dialectics*, trans. E. B. Ashton, New York: Seabury Press, 1973, 197.

link with the proletariat, and asserted the primacy of the economy, writ large.[15] Forty years later, Herbert Marcuse, who in the thirties was one of the rising stars of the Institute, would argue that 'to the end, Marxist theory itself was [its] integrating force'.[16]

Critical theory – as opposed to 'traditional theory', first laid out in Descartes' *Discourse on Method* (1637) and embodied in the 'special disciplines' [*Fachwissenschaften*] – first of all rejected the intellectual division of labour, and with it all existing conceptions of theory, in the social as well as the natural sciences, whether empiricist or not. It is a 'human stance [*menschliches Verhalten*]', wrote Horkheimer, 'that has society itself as its object'. The vocation of the critical theorist 'is the struggle, to which his thinking belongs'. Critical theory is 'one single elaborate existential judgement'.[17] While rejecting a role in the existing division of labour, critical theorists do not stand outside or above classes. Between them and 'the ruled class' exists 'a dynamic unity', although that unity 'exists only as conflict'. Through the interaction between the theorist and the ruled class, the process of social change may be accelerated. The task of critical theory is to contribute to 'the transformation of the social whole', which will occur only through ever sharper social conflicts. The theory, therefore, offers neither short-term amelioration nor gradual material improvements. Nevertheless, critical theory is theory, characterized by formal conceptualization, deductive logic and experiential reference. Individual parts of it may also operate in 'traditional' modes of thought, that is, in ordinary scientific analyses. It is

---

15. M. Horkheimer, 'Traditionelle und kritische Theorie', 187ff; and 'Nachtrag' (1937), in M. Horkheimer, *Gesammelte schriften*, vol. 4, 222.

16. See J. Habermas, *The Theory of Communicative Action*, trans. T. McCarthy, Boston: Beacon Press, 1981, 197.

17. M. Horkheimer, 'Traditionelle und kritische Theorie', 180, 190, 201.

neither hostile to nor uninterested in empirical research.[18]

The core of critical theory as theory is the Marxian concept of exchange, out of which developed the 'real, world-encompassing capitalist society' in Europe.[19] Critical theory is 'in many places' reduced to economism, but that does not mean that the economic is regarded as too important, rather that it is taken too narrowly. The process of social formation [*Vergesellschaftung*], if it is taking place, needs to be studied and analyzed not only in narrow economic terms, but also with regard to the functioning of the state, and to the development of 'essential moments of real democracy and association'.[20] 'It would be false', wrote Marcuse, 'to dissolve the economic concepts into philosophical ones. Rather, on the contrary . . . relevant philosophical objects are to be developed from the economic context.'[21]

It may be pertinent to briefly compare critical theory in its original, classical form with another programmatic formulation of the place and use of social knowledge from a radical viewpoint, written almost simultaneously with Horkheimer's text, and in the same city, by a professor at Columbia University, which also served as a host for the Frankfurt Institute in exile. Robert Lynd's *Knowledge for What?* appeared in 1939, as the printed version of a lecture series at Princeton in the spring of 1938. The concerns and the long-term sociopolitical perspectives of the German philosopher and the American sociologist are, in many respects, similar. Lynd is also critical of the academic division of labour. He criticizes empirical social science's tendency to take contemporary institutions for

---

18. Ibid., 192–3, 199–200. The critical theorists' very wide-ranging interest in empirical research comes out most clearly in the contents of the *Zeitschrift für Sozialforschung*, the journal of the Institute.
19. Ibid., 201.
20. M. Horkheimer, 'Nachtrag', 222–3.
21. H. Marcuse, 'Philosophie und kritische Theorie', 102.

granted. Instead, Lynd wants to orient it to 'what the present human carriers of those institutions are groping to become', i.e., to institutional change.[22] The direction of such change to which Lynd commits himself is also similar to Horkheimer's, namely, the 'marked' extension of democracy, not only in government but also in industry and other forms of endeavour, and the replacement of 'private capitalism'.[23]

But the language and the mode of thought are very different. Lynd does not fall back on a theoretical tradition, but argues from the perspective of the empirical issues of the day. His pragmatic conception of social science – 'Social science will stand or fall on the basis of its serviceability to men as they struggle to live'[24] – is viewed by Horkheimer with a sceptical frown. His historical-critical perspective is not one of exploitation and class – although he does argue that class and class conflict deserve much more consideration by US social scientists – but a sort of anthropology of 'human cravings', as a yardstick for appraising existing institutions.[25] Lynd's socialism is not a vocation of struggle, but presents itself as the 'hypothesis' that capitalism 'does not operate and probably cannot be made to operate, to assure the amount of general welfare to which the present stage of our technical skills and intelligence entitle us'.[26]

The different critical idiom typical of American radicalism was carried on after Lynd most characteristically and influentially by C. Wright Mills in *The Sociological Imagination* (1959). The three basic questions of that imagination, which Mills took on with the obvious self-confidence and

22. R.S. Lynd, *Knowledge for What?*, Princeton, NJ: Princeton University Press, 1939, 180, emphasis omitted.
23. Ibid., 220.
24. Ibid., 177.
25. Ibid., 192ff.
26. Ibid., 220.

straightforward directness of the New World craftsman, were the same as those underlying most of the more convoluted, as well as much more elaborate and subtle, social reflections of the Frankfurt School: 'What is the structure of this particular society as a whole?', 'Where does this society stand in human history? What are the mechanics by which it is changing?' and 'What varieties of men and women now prevail in this society and in this period?'[27] Adorno, Horkheimer, Marcuse et al. would, of course, have turned away in disgust at the notion of a 'mechanics' of historical change. On the other hand, Mills's fast-paced prose attached no special interpretation of history to the word. The critical theorists also pursued other interests than social theory, including the theory of knowledge and the history of theory, among other things.

POPPER VERSUS ADORNO

In 1961 the German Sociological Association confronted a thorough and fundamentally antagonistic critique when it invited Karl Popper to give an address on the logic of the social sciences, with Adorno as respondent. The formal encounter was polite, but in Germany a heated controversy ensued which, to the anger of Sir Karl, became known as the *Positivismusstreit* – the positivism controversy.[28] Popper, who rejected the 'positivist' label, presented his viewpoint as 'criticist', the nucleus of which is a view of scientific method as consisting of 'tentative attempts at solutions' to the problems tackled, solutions controlled by 'the sharpest criticism'. Popper explicitly attacked an

---

27. C. W. Mills, *The Sociological Imagination*, New York: Galaxy/Oxford University Press, 1967 (1959), 6.
28. K. R. Popper, 'The Frankfurt School: An Autobiographical Note', in *Foundations of the Frankfurt School of Social Research*, J. Marcus and Z. Tar, eds, New Brunswick: Transaction books, 1984; T. Adorno et al., *The Positivist Dispute in German Sociology*, trans. D. Adey and G. Frisby, London: Heinemann, 1976.

inductivist and naturalist conception of science, and recognized the value of an interpretative method of the 'logic of the situation' in the social sciences.[29]

As a dialectician, Adorno found, to his surprise, many things to agree with in Popper's criticist position, and his argument was more a further reflection on Popper's theses than the presentation of a set of antitheses. This did not, however, blunt his characteristic critical edge.[30] Adorno's main divergence from Popper concerned the object of criticism or critique – in German, the same word is used for both. For Popper, the target of criticism was proposed solutions to scientific problems, but for Adorno critique had to extend to the totality of society. Only when we can conceive of society as being different from what it is does the present society become a problem for us: 'only through what it is not will it disclose itself as it is, and that, I would assume, is what it comes to in a sociology, which does not, like most of its projects, true, limit itself to purposes of public and private administration.'[31]

The dialectic of critical theory developed beyond the

29. K. R. Popper, 'Die Logik der Sozialwissenschaften', in *Der Positivismusstreit in der deutschen Soziologie*, H. Maus and F. Fürstenberg, eds, Neuwied and Berlin: Luchterhand 1962, 106–7, 120.

30. T. Adorno, 'Zur Logik der Sozialwissenschaften', in *Der Positivismusstreit in der deutschen Soziologie*, 125, 128. The contrast between the elegant fencing of Adorno and the unpleasant after-the-event arrogance of Popper comes through in Adorno's abstinence from any personal attacks in his 1969 introduction as well as in his 1961 *Korreferat*. At the end of the latter, Adorno referred to a correspondence preceding the meeting, in which Popper should have said that the difference between him and Adorno might be that he, Popper, believed that they lived in the best of worlds but Adorno did not. While saying that the evil of societies was always difficult to judge, and that he was equally hostile to a 'standpoint' theory, Adorno admitted that he found it difficult to assume that there had been no better epoch than the one which had spawned Auschwitz. See ibid., 141–2. Popper afterwards gave vent to a tirade of invective, which may be summed up as: Adorno 'has nothing whatever to say; and he says it in Hegelian language'. Popper, 'The Frankfurt School', 167.

31. Ibid., 142.

Marxian critique of political economy. During the war, Horkheimer abandoned his plan to write a major treatise on dialectics; instead he and Adorno put together a collection of essays and fragments, *Dialectic of Enlightenment* (1944). The theme set the tone for the postwar Frankfurt School – namely, the self-destruction of the Enlightenment written from a commitment to 'salvaging the enlightenment'.[32] This was still seen as an extension of Marxism, but Friedrich Pollock's interpretation of Fascism as state capitalism, of which Stalinism was also a variant, tended to push the classical Marxian economic categories into the background, a process which is already evident in the changes between the unpublished 1944 version of *Dialectic of Enlightenment* and the 1947 Amsterdam edition.[33] Horkheimer's last major work, *The Eclipse of Reason* (1947), centred on the critique of instrumental reason. After the war, when Adorno became the foremost critical theorist, 'die verwaltete Welt', the tragic timbre of which is unmusically rendered in English as 'the administered world', became a central critical concept. Freud and his cultural critique were also incorporated in postwar critical theory, most elaborately in Herbert Marcuse's *Eros and Civilization* (1955).

Yet the umbilical cord to the Marxian critique of political economy was never cut, even if little hope of any positive dialectical outcome remained. This critique provided the baseline for Marcuse's critique of 'the ideology of industrial society'.[34] It was present in Adorno's polemic with Popper, and it was eminently present in

---

32. M. Horkheimer and T. Adorno, *Dialektik der Aufklärung* (1944), in Horkheimer, *Gesammelte Schriften*, vol. 5, 597.

33. W. van Reijen and J. Braunsen, 'Das Verschwinden der Klassengeschichte in der *Dialektik der Aufklärung*: Ein Kommentar zu den Textvarianten der Buchausgabe von 1947 gegenüber der Erstveröffentlichung von 1944', in Horkheimer, *Gesammelte Schriften*, vol. 5.

34. H. Marcuse, *One-Dimensional Man: Studies in the Ideology of Advanced Industrial Society*, Boston: Beacon, 1964.

Adorno's final work, his spring 1968 lectures presenting an introduction to sociology. Here he took C. Wright Mills to task for remaining so tied to the ruling conventions of sociology that he neglected the analysis of economic processes.[35]

HABERMAS'S NEW TERRAIN

By 1968, however, Jürgen Habermas, Adorno's assistant and protégé and Horkheimer's successor to the Frankfurt chair of philosophy and sociology, was already at work, taking the critical project out of Marxian political economy. These new developments were originally motivated by changes in capitalism itself, which produced new roles for politics, science and technology. For the Marxian concepts of forces and relations of production – the key concepts of Marx's theory of the social dialectic – Habermas substituted 'labour', which involved both instrumental action and rational choice, and 'symbolically mediated interaction' or 'communicative action'. In a series of lectures and essays in the course of the 1960s, Habermas laid out a new theoretical terrain,[36] on which he was later to erect his great theoretical constructions, his *Theory of Communicative Action* and his theory of law.[37] Habermas abandoned the systemic contradiction analyzed by Marxist theory, replacing it first with a distinction between different kinds of action and knowledge interests, and later with a conflict between the social system and the 'life-world'.

In spite of some quite valid claims to legitimacy, Habermas has not seen or presented himself, or even without objection allowed others to present him, as the

---

35. T. Adorno, *Einleitung in die Soziologie*, ed. C. Gödde, Frankfurt: Suhrkamp, 1993, 237–8.

36. J. Habermas, *Technik und Wissenschaft als 'Ideologie'*, Frankfurt: Suhrkamp 1968.

37. J. Habermas, *Theory of Communicative Action*.

heir of critical theory, or as continuing the work of the Frankfurt School. On the other hand, 'critical social theory' of a wider sort is something which he has continued to practice 'in an unreservedly self-correcting and self-critical mode'.[38] A critical defence of modernity has remained central to that practice.[39] Historically or sociologically, there remains, then, across all differences of substantial theory, an affinity between Marx and Habermas.[40]

Habermas broke not only with the critique of political economy, but with the discourse of his predecessors in other ways. He has abandoned their 'fragmentary' *Essaïstik* for elaborate critical confrontations with other modes of thought. Indeed, Habermas's way of developing his work through long presentations and discussions of work by others resembles Marx more than Adorno. His conceptions of communicative rationality and 'domination-free communication' constitute an attempt to provide a normative foundation for his own critical position, something with which neither Adorno, Horkheimer nor Marcuse, steeped in the classical tradition of German idealism, never bothered.[41]

Critical theory is a philosophical reception of, reflection on and elaboration of Marx's critique of political economy,

---

38. J. Habermas, 'Critical Theory and Frankfurt University', in *Autonomy and Solidarity*, ed. P. Dews, London: Verso, 1992, 212.

39. J. Habermas, *The Philosophical Discourse of Modernity*, trans. F. Lawrence, Cambridge: MIT Press, 1985; and *Die Moderne – ein unvollendetes Projekt*, Leipzig: Reclam, 1992.

40. A quarter of a century ago, the differences of substance appeared paramount to someone who, from the viewpoint of an Anglo-Saxon and Scandinavian student and young academic, wanted to establish the legitimacy of Marxist theory where, prior to 1968, this was institutionally denied. I still think the distinctions made then were correct with regard to content, and even that a defence of Marxism at that time was a positive contribution to social thought as critique, as well as science. However, the dismissive polemical tone adopted then, now appears jejune. See G. Therborn, 'Jürgen Habermas: A New Eclecticism', *New Left Review 1:* 67, May–June 1971, 69–83.

41. See J. Habermas, 'Ideologies and Society in the Postwar World', in *Autonomy and Solidarity*, 56.

set in the context of the traumatic events between 1914 and 1989, from the slaughter of the First World War, the abortive revolution in the West and its crippled birth in Russia, the Depression, and the victory of Fascism – with its institutionalization and rationalization of the pogrom that was the Holocaust – to the rise of Big Organizations, the Second World War and the one-dimensionality of the Cold War. In its own very special tonality, critical theory expresses a strand of radical reflexivity in the European road through modernity.

Critical theory's classical texts were written on the run, in exile from the machinery of annihilation, in obscure editions and increasingly in code. They were hidden from view in the 1950s and 1960s, not only by competing world-views but also by the critical theorists themselves.[42] When critical theory resurfaced, it was in the context of media-prominent anti-colonial revolts and the rise of a mass student body, and the classical texts were for the first time published for a wide audience.[43] The reception had its special irony: the encounter of a young generation of revolutionary hope with an old one of revolutionary defeat, holding out against hope. The affinity was closest with radical American academia, which always had much less reason to harbour any practical hope than its European comrades. To the latter, practice held out more promise than critique, whether

---

42. Habermas, who in the late fifties was Adorno's assistant, has told us that the *Zeitschrift für Sozialforschung*, the 1930s journal of the Institute, was kept in a locked coffer in the basement of the Institute. Until 1968 Horkheimer also refused the entreaties of his publisher, S. Fischer, to republish his prewar essays in book form. In spite of his triumphal return to Germany, becoming rector of the Goethe University in Frankfurt and Honorary Citizen of the city, Horkheimer insisted on and managed to keep an American passport and an Institute retreat in New York. See 'Max Horkheimer: Die Frankfurter Schule in New York', in J. Habermas, *Philosophisch-politische Profile*, Frankfurt: Suhrkamp, 1981, 415.
43. M. Horkheimer's two-volume Fischer edition of *Kritische Theorie* in 1968, and T. Adorno's and M. Horkheimer's *Dialektik der Aufklärung* in 1969, also by Fischer.

the practice of the existing working-class and labour movements or the practice of guidance by the new vanguards
being constructed.

THE RELEVANCE OF THE FRANKFURT SCHOOL REVIVED

Now, in this second fin-de-siècle, the Frankfurt moment
has returned. Adorno's words are much closer to the radical
mood of 2008 than that of 1968: 'Philosophy, which once
seemed obsolete, lives on because the moment to realize
it was missed. The summary judgement that it had merely
interpreted the world . . . becomes a defeatism of reason
after the attempt to change the world had miscarried.'[44]
To people of the twenty-first century, the critical critique
by the 'Holy Family' of the early 1840s might appear closer
than the later Marxian critique of political economy. Bruno
Bauer's concerns – 'The Jewish Question', 'The Good
Thing of Freedom', 'State, Religion and Party' – sound
more familiar than those of Engels and Marx – 'revolution,
materialism, socialism, communism'.[45]

In any case, in this context, critical theory is a metonym.
The original editorial assignment of critical theory was
something much broader than critical theory in the literal
sense, namely, 'the legacy of Marxism'. While twentieth-
century Marxism is infinitely richer and broader than the
tiny Western intellectual coterie that promulgates critical
theory, it might be argued that, for all its limitations,
critical theory has been the grandchild of Marx that
most explicitly and persistently expressed an aspect of
the historical quintessence of Marxism – its reflection on
the dialectics of modernity. Marxism's sombre thinkers of

---

44. T. Adorno, *Negative Dialectics*, 3.
45. F. Engels and K. Marx, *Die heilige Familie oder Kritik der kritischen Kritik*
(1844), in *Marx-Engels Werke*, vol. 2.

the negative dialectic who embraced individualist refusal, Adorno and Marcuse in particular, capture this dialectic no less and no more than the positive class dialectic held out by Karl Kautsky's *The Social Revolution* (1902) and *The Road to Power* (1909). Kautsky represents one perspective, while *Dialectic of Enlightenment, Minima Moralia, Negative Dialectics* and *One-Dimensional Man* represent another.[46]

Critical theory is usually regarded as part of a larger subdivision of twentieth-century Marxism called 'Western Marxism', a term launched in the mid-1950s by Maurice Merleau-Ponty, who has sometimes been included in it himself.[47] 'Western Marxism' has generally been treated as a pantheon of individuals and individual works that express a certain intellectual mood, rather than as a tradition or a movement. The set of Western Marxists has always been fuzzy, although by general agreement, the current started after the October Revolution, as a Western European reaction to it, a positive but special reaction, beginning with Georg Lukács's *History and Class Consciousness* and Karl Korsch's *Marxism and Philosophy*, both published in 1923 in German. Lukács was a German-educated Hungarian philosopher and aesthetician, and Korsch a German professor of law. Both were prominent Communists in the abortive revolutions in Hungary and Germany, both were criticized as leftists and philosophical deviants by their comrades, and Korsch was excluded from the German Communist Party in 1925. In creating the label of Western Marxism, Merleau-Ponty took his cue from Korsch, who ironically referred to Soviet criticism of himself, Lukács and two other Hungarian intellectuals,

---

46. T. Adorno, *Minima Moralia*, trans. E.F.N. Jephcott, London: New Left Books, 1974; T. Adorno, *Negative Dialectics*; H. Marcuse, *One-Dimensional Man*.

47. M. Merleau-Ponty, *Les aventures de la dialectique*, Paris: Gallimard, 1955, chaps. 2 and 3.

Jozef Revái and Bela Fogarasi.[48] Merleau-Ponty applied it mainly to Lukács, contrasting his work, strongly influenced by Max Weber, to the orthodox Communist tradition, particularly Lenin's *Materialism and Empirio-Criticism* (1908). It is generally agreed that another distinguished member of the first generation was Antonio Gramsci, who became the leader of the Italian Communist Party in 1924. Most of his written work is contained in his *Notebooks*, which include a wide range of lucid and original political, cultural and social analyses, penned whilst incarcerated in a Fascist prison from 1926 onwards. Perhaps his most famous article dealt with the October Revolution. It first appeared on 24 November 1917 under the title 'The Revolution Against *Capital*': 'The revolution of the Bolsheviks has materialized out of ideologies rather than facts ... This is the revolution against the *Capital* of Karl Marx.'[49]

WESTERN AND OTHER MARXISMS

A sociologist of knowledge or an ecumenical historian of ideas might define Western Marxism as a politically autonomous Marxist trend of thought in the advanced capitalist countries after the October Revolution. As such, it is differentiated both from the Marxisms of other parts of the world and from the practically institutionalized

---

48. Korsch himself did not attach any importance to the label, to which he refers only obliquely, with ironic quotation marks. See *Marxisme et philosophie* (1923), trans. K. Axelos, Paris: Éditions de Minuit, 1964, 40. The main Soviet critic of Lukács and 'his disciples', Abram Deborin ('Lukács und seine Kritik des Marxismus' (1924), in *Kontroversen über dialektischen und mechanistischen Materialismus*, ed. O. Negt, Frankfurt: Suhrkamp, 1969, 192 and passim), does not use it at all. And what Korsch ironically referred to was not Western Marxism but '"Western" Communists'. It might also be added that the Soviet polemic with Lukács, Korsch, Revái, et al. took place before Stalinism. Korsch's main work, *Marxism and Philosophy*, appeared in two editions in the USSR in 1924.
49. A. Gramsci, 'La rivoluzione contro il *Capitale*' (1917), in G. Gerrata and N. Gallo, eds, *2000 Pagine di Gramsci*, vol. 1, Milan: Il Saggiatore, 1964, 265.

Marxism of parties or political groupings. However, Western Marxism is a *post hoc* construction, having a particular meaning even in the least partisan and most erudite versions. Starting from the latter, as significant definitions, we shall here try to situate the phenomenon connoted by 'Western Marxism' somewhat differently, from a more distant vantage-point.

The best treatments of Western Marxism have tended to work from rosters of individuals. Thus, Perry Anderson lists, in order of age, Georg Lukács (b. 1885), Karl Korsch, Antonio Gramsci, Walter Benjamin, Max Horkheimer, Galvano Della Volpe, Herbert Marcuse, Henri Lefebvre, Theodor W. Adorno, Jean-Paul Sartre, Lucien Goldmann, Louis Althusser and Lucio Colletti (b. 1924).[50] The defining boundary is, first of all, generational. Western Marxism thus consists of a set of theorists who matured politically and theoretically only after the First World War, but whose positions consolidated after the Second. To Anderson, 'the hidden hallmark' of Western Marxism is defeat, a characteristic which is intelligible only in terms of his somewhat specialized periodization. He also contrasts Western Marxism with Trotskyism, of which he designates Ernest Mandel as a theoretically eminent exponent.

Martin Jay sees Western Marxism as 'created by a loose circle of theorists who took their cue from Lukács and the other founding fathers of the immediate post-World War I era, Antonio Gramsci, Karl Korsch, and Ernst Bloch'.[51] After Adorno, Benjamin, Horkheimer and Marcuse, he adds Leo Löwenthal (also of the Frankfurt School) and Maurice Merleau-Ponty, and points out that the following

were frequently admitted to their ranks: Bertolt Brecht, Wilhelm Reich, Erich Fromm, the Council

50. P. Anderson, *Considerations on Western Marxism*, London: New Left Books, 1976, 25–6.
51. M. Jay, *Marxism and Totality*, Berkeley: University of California Press, 1984, 3.

Communists in Holland (Herman Gorter, Anton Pannekoek and others), the *Arguments* group in France (in the late 1950s, Kostas Axelos, Edgar Morin and others), and second-generation Frankfurt School members like Jürgen Habermas and Alfred Schmidt. And still others like Alfred Sohn-Rethel, Leo Kofler, Franz Jakubowski, Claude Lefort and Cornelius Castoriadis.[52]

While pointing out that Western Marxism had previously meant largely Hegelian Marxism, Jay basically accepts Anderson's more sociological definition.

From these roll-calls, certain broad themes have emerged. Merleau-Ponty wanted to remind his readers of 'the youth of revolution and of Marxism' manifested by Lukács's 'lively and vigorous essay', its contrast to a scientific conception of Marxism, its attention to the 'superstructure', and its inability to 'express the inertia of the infrastructures, of the resistance of economic and even natural conditions, of how "personal relations" become bogged down [*l'enlisement*] in "things" '.[53]

Anderson highlights the shifts of these intellectuals from work on politics, economics and labour-movement institutions to academia and philosophy. After the Second World War, all the survivors – Gramsci and Benjamin had, in different ways, been hunted to death by Fascist regimes[54] – were academic philosophers of professorial rank, except Sartre, who had left a budding academic career to be a

---

52. The last two, who became quite influential in France after 1968, were the key figures of a splinter from Trotskyism, a group and a journal published in 1949–65 called *Socialisme ou Barbarie*, from which also came the later theorist of postmodernism Jean-François Lyotard.

53. M. Merleau-Ponty, *Les aventures de la dialectique*, 80, 88.

54. Gramsci's frail health was finally broken, in 1937, by nine years in Italian imprisonment. Benjamin killed himself while on the run from the Nazis, in 1940.

writer. The movement's 'most striking single trait . . . as a common tradition is . . . perhaps the constant pressure and influence on it of successive types of European idealism'. The work of the Western Marxists concentrated particularly on epistemology and aesthetics, while also making thematic innovations in Marxist discourse, among which Anderson stresses Gramsci's concept of hegemony, the Frankfurt vision of liberation as a reconciliation with, rather than a domination of, nature, and the recourse to Freud. Running through all these innovations is a 'common and latent pessimism'.[55]

Martin Jay's work uses the concept of totality as his 'compass' through the territory of Western Marxism. Jay explicitly refrains from arguing that totality is the only possible compass for such purposes, but since it was emphasized by Lukács, it has certainly been at the centre of Western Marxism and has been submitted to various definitions, elaborations and applications, which Jay pursues with great skill.

REREADING WESTERN MARXISM IN RETROSPECT

However defined, 'Western Marxism' is a *Nachkonstruktion*, a *post hoc* construction, not a self-recognized group or current. Nevertheless, a somewhat more distanced perspective than those of Merleau-Ponty, Anderson and Jay makes possible a somewhat different historical positioning of Western Marxism, namely, as another historical reading open to empirical falsification.

If we take Lukács as the key figure, and *History and Class Consciousness* as the central text, which seems non-controversial, we can locate the origin of Western Marxism with some exactitude.[56] The original text was

---

55. P. Anderson, *Considerations on Western Marxism*, 56, 88, emphasis omitted.
56. G. Lukács, *History and Class Consciousness*, trans. R. Livingstone, London: Merlin Press Ltd, 1971.

written in 1918, before Lukács joined the new Hungarian Communist Party. It is called 'Bolshevism as a Moral Problem'. It poses with exemplary lucidity the issue of its title:

> whether democracy is believed to be a temporary tactic of the socialist movement, a useful tool to be employed . . . or if democracy indeed is an integral part of socialism. If the latter is true, democracy cannot be forsaken without considering the ensuing moral and ideological consequences.
>
>   Bolshevism offers a fascinating way out in that it does not call for compromise. But all those who fall under the sway of its fascination might not be fully aware of the consequences of their decision . . . Is it possible to achieve good by condemnable means? Can freedom be attained by means of oppression?[57]

In that article, Lukács left the questions hanging, but his Western Marxism was an oblique way of answering 'yes' to the last two.

In 1918 Lukács was not at all attached to 'Western Marxism' in the sense of his 1923 book and its later reception – indeed, his views were diametrically opposed to it. 'In the past', Lukács wrote in 1918,

> Marx's philosophy of history has seldom been sufficiently separated from his sociology. As a result, it has often been overlooked that the two constitutive elements of his system, class struggle and socialism . . . are closely related but by no means the product of the same conceptual system. The former is a factual finding of Marxian sociology . . . Socialism, on the

---

57. G. Lukács, 'Bolshevism as a Moral Problem' (1918), trans. J. Marcus, *Social Research* 44: 3, 1977, 419, 423.

other hand, is the utopian postulate of the Marxian philosophy of history: it is the ethical objective of a coming world order.[58]

This is a Marxism filtered by neo-Kantianism, very much present in the Max Weber circle in Heidelberg of which Lukács was then a part, and grafted onto an orthodox, in part left-wing, Marxism by Max Adler and the whole tendency of 'Austro-Marxism', which had developed in Vienna in the decade prior to the First World War and included Otto Bauer, Rudolf Hilferding, Karl Renner and others in its ranks.

The birth of Western Marxism consisted in conflating, or, if you prefer, transcending, the distinction between science and ethics with a Hegelian dialectic of class consciousness. Its first adumbration is Lukács's first article after his return to Hungary as a Communist, 'Tactics and Ethics', though the article was written before the short-lived Soviet Republic. Here, morally correct action is made dependent on knowledge of the 'historical philosophical situation', on class consciousness. It ends on a note, later expanded, particularly in the key essay *History and Class Consciousness*, on reification and the consciousness of the proletariat: 'This calling to the salvation of society is the world-historical role of the proletariat and only through the class consciousness of the proletarians can you reach the knowledge and the understanding of this road of humanity.'[59]

The immediate target in Karl Korsch's *Marxism and Philosophy*, the second canonical text of Western Marxism, is Austro-Marxism, exemplified by Rudolf Hilferding and his *Finance Capital* (1909), which is attacked in the

58. Ibid., 420, emphasis omitted.
59. G. Lukács, 'Taktik und Ethik' (1919), trans. M. Leszák and P. Ludz, in *Soziologische Texte*, ed. P. Ludz, Neuwied and Berlin: Luchterhand, 1967, 19.

name of a Hegelian dialectic that rejects Austro-Marxism's dissolution of the 'unitary theory of social revolution' into scientific study and political *prises de position*.[60]

CRITICAL THEORY AND THE OCTOBER REVOLUTION

On the basis of this brief sketch – a documentation which could and should have been largely extended in a more specialized context – we may draw some conclusions. Western Marxism arose as a European intellectual reception of the October Revolution. The latter was interpreted as a successful abbreviation of Marxist thought, against *Capital* and against facts according to Gramsci, overcoming both moral and scientific problems according to Lukács and Korsch. Hailing the October Revolution also meant, of course, hailing Lenin's leadership, to which Lukács paid homage in 1919,[61] and from whom Korsch borrowed the motto of his *Marxism and Philosophy*. To link Western Marxism with 'the anti-Leninist movement of this century' is American leftists' 'false consciousness'.[62]

On the other hand, the construction, diffusion and perception of a Western Marxism by Western European intellectuals in the late 1950s and 1960s, and by North Americans somewhat later, always implied an Eastern demarcation. The 'East', against which Western Marxism was implicitly contrasted, was seen in many different forms, but clearly included the Communist Party canon and the rival orthodoxies of Soviet post-Stalinism, Sino-Stalinism, Maoism and organized Trotskyism. The main function of 1960s Western Marxism was to open up an intellectual horizon and a field of reflection, where theoretical and conceptual issues

---

60. K. Korsch, *Marxisme et philosophie*, 92ff.
61. L. Lukács, 'Taktik und Ethik', 19.
62. S. Aronowitz, *The Crisis in Historical Materialism: Class, Politics and Culture in Marxist Theory*, Minneapolis: University of Minnesota Press, 1981, xiii.

could be discussed without being foreclosed by party-line polemics or divisive political loyalties.

While it is true that the prospect of revolution west of Russia receded after 1923, I do not think it is very illuminating to characterize Western Marxism as a theory marked by defeat. Not only was this obviously untrue of its founding moment, but Anderson's characterization now appears to take too narrow or specialist an angle. Rather, all the members of his list became Marxists because they regarded the October Revolution as a decisive, world-historical event. Of the thirteen names on Anderson's list, seven were Communists – lifelong adherents, indeed, except for Korsch and Colletti. The Horkheimer circle, with four members on Anderson's list, always stayed aloof from tangible political connections, but was clearly sympathetic to the USSR before the Second World War and afterwards never heeded the sirens of Cold War anti-Communist mobilization. Adorno and Horkheimer both sneered at the authoritarian regimes in Eastern Europe but without openly denouncing them, and Herbert Marcuse wrote a sober and scholarly critical study of *Soviet Marxism* (1963) which ended by pointing out the rational, and potentially critical, aspect of Soviet social philosophy. The remaining two, Goldmann and Sartre, also moved in the orbit of the October Revolution – Goldmann as a fervent disciple of the young Lukács, Sartre circling the French Communist Party at varying distances, but in the postwar period always within the circuit of proletarian revolution.

Because of the importance of the October Revolution and the USSR to the two classical generations of Western Marxism, I think it makes most sense to draw a line after the recent death of Henri Lefebvre, in mid-1991. While there are a number of figures of the '1968 generation' who might be called into service or who might rally to a continuation of something they would call Western Marxism, no one has, or could possibly have, the same relationship to the possibility of a working-class revolution or to any remotely similar mixture of faith and disillusion. The way Habermas, Adorno's former assistant, broke out of the 'tacit orthodoxy' of the Frankfurt School onto new ground exemplifies this.

THE PHILOSOPHICAL TURN

This account has not dealt with the question of whether all or most Western Marxists were philosophers, and, if so, why. Here the lists of Anderson, Jay, Merleau-Ponty and others are, at best, as reliable as the verdict of an academic nominating committee, which, as every academic knows, is a qualified compliment. It may be that Anderson's argument is circular. All his names, with the possible and partial exceptions of Benjamin and Gramsci, are philosophers, but how do we know that individuals other than philosophers stood a fair chance of joining the list? Jay's roster is also philosopher-dominated.[63] The absence of social scientists and historians is virtually complete. Yet, given the *post hoc* construction of 'Western Marxism', what we see here, I would suggest, is the interaction of two factors: the intellectual climate in Europe at the time of the reception of the October Revolution, and the later Western European and North American image of 'Western Marxism'. In other words, philosophers were prevalent in 1917, and latter-day Marxists have wanted to listen to philosophers.

It should first be remembered that a number of intellectual paths and careers were not open to those who identified early with the October Revolution. Empirical social science was little – if at all – established in Europe.

---

63. Sohn-Rethel might be called an economic historican, though Brecht was a playwright, Reich and Fromm were above all psychoanalysts, and among the Dutch Council Communists, Gorter was a poet and Pannekoek an astronomer.

Sociology remained strung between 'the politics of the bourgeois revolutions and the economics of the proletarian revolution', and lived a precarious institutional existence.[64] Economics departments were usually hostile to the critique of economics. Political science was only beginning to move into social studies of politics. Law faculties covered much of what would later branch out into social disciplines, but were still dominated by venerable tradition. Historiography was still overwhelmingly hostile to any social-scientific intrusion.

It seems that in the heartlands of Europe, philosophy was the academic discipline most open to people who had welcomed the dawn of October 1917. Philosophy was relatively remote from the powers and interests of the day; in addition, it was clearly non-paradigmatic, harbouring a number of schools. It was the medium in which the most general and important issues of humankind were discussed – life, history, knowledge, morals. But, like twentieth-century philosophers in general, Marxist philosophers tended over time to move in the direction of sociology, though usually without abandoning their academic origins. After the Second World War, this sociological turn is clearly discernible in Adorno, Horkheimer and Marcuse, in Henri Lefebvre and his original comrade Georges Friedmann, and in Sartre.[65]

But, however defined, Western Marxism is, of course, only one strand of twentieth-century Marxism. Furthermore,

---

64. G. Therborn, *Science, Class and Society*, London: New Left Books, 1976.
65. Adorno and the Frankfurt Institute went into social psychology and group and industrial sociology; Henri Lefebvre embarked upon a philosophical sociology of 'everyday life' (*Critique de la vie quotidienne*, 2 vols, Paris: Grasset, 1948–61). Friedmann became, one might say, the founder of French industrial sociology. Sartre was concerned with demonstrating the value of the dialectical method to the 'sciences of man', which involved a running critical dialogue with existing sociology, as Sartre saw it (*Critique de la raison dialectique*, Paris: Editions Gallimard, 1960, 153). Maurice Godelier went from philosophy to anthropology. In 1964, the Gramsci Institute in Italy organized an important symposium on Marxism and sociology.

any critical perspective on the latter must take into account that Marxism is not a self-contained universe of its own theories, practices and polemics. Marxism, and with it critical theory, has been part of an intellectual and sociopolitical history, with alternatives, rivals and opponents. Within such a history, the proper location of critical theory in the narrow or specific sense can be ascertained.

MARXISM AND THE ROUTES THROUGH MODERNITY

Marxism is not just any old theoretical corpus. As a distinctive cognitive perspective on the modern world, it is surpassed in social significance – in terms of numbers of adherents – only by the great world religions. As a modern pole of identity, it is outdistanced only by nationalism.[66] Marxism acquired its very special historical importance by becoming, from the 1880s till the 1970s,[67] the main intellectual culture of two major social movements of the dialectics of modernity: the labour movement and the anticolonial movement. In neither case was Marxism without important rivals, nor was its diffusion universal, uniform or without defeats. But none of its competitors had a comparable reach and persistence.

Marxism was also significant to feminism, from the times of Clara Zetkin and Alexandra Kollontai to those of Simone de Beauvoir and, later, Juliet Mitchell, Frigga Haug and Michèle Barrett. But in spite of their uniquely profeminist stance among male-dominated movements, Marxist parties and currents were regularly overshadowed

---

66. There is not yet a study quite level with this enormous subject. But the best there is, which is excellent in many of its contributions, particularly by the main editor himself, is Eric Hobsbawm et al., *Storia del marxismo*, 4 vols, Turin: Einaudi, 1978–82.

67. As far as the labour movement in the most developed capitalist countries is concerned, the *terminus ad quem* is rather the 1960s.

by religious and other conservative movements when it came to attracting mass support among women.

Marxism had its origin in Europe, and its dialectical conception of history corresponded best to the European route to and through modernity, the road of endogenous change through fully internal conflicts between forces for and against modernity, however conceived. Within European modernity, Marxism gained where competing forces for the allegiance of the working class were weak and had become discredited by defeat. To its immediate right was liberalism or, in the Latin countries, radicalism. In Britain the former was strong and vigorous; in France and, to some extent, in the Iberian peninsula, the latter. On the right also was Christian democracy, but it began after Marxism and became important only in countries with strong churches that were autonomous from the state bureaucracy, which meant the Catholic Church in the Low Countries, the Rhineland, Southern Germany and Italy, and the militant (*Gereformeerde*) Calvinist churches of the Netherlands. To Marxism's left were anarchism, anarchosyndicalism and Russian populism. The anarchists were soon marginalized in most places except Andalusia; the anarchosyndicalists were largely defeated in Italy and France, holding on mainly in Spain; and the populists suffered severe defeats in late nineteenth-century Russia. The Marxist strongholds were Central – running north–south from Scandinavia to central Italy – and Eastern Europe, where a working class was being formed without prior modern ideological experience. In autocratic Russia, with little intellectual freedom of expression for any modern ideas, Marxism became, after the defeats of populism, the main language of the intelligentsia. German social democracy was the undisputed centre of gravity of European, and world, Marxism before 1914. German was Marxism's main language, either directly or as the source of translation, even in countries whose cultural orientation was predominantly Russian, such as Serbia or Bulgaria, or French, such as Romania. Karl Kautsky's *Die Neue Zeit* (*New Times*) was the leading journal.

The First World War and its end had a strong but complex effect on European Marxism. The October Revolution attracted a significant cohort of workers and intellectuals to Marxism, and the new Communist parties started a vigorous programme of publication and diffusion of works by Marx and Engels. In Germany a certain academic opening occurred, particularly in social-democratically-governed Prussia, to which Frankfurt belonged. But the Marxism of social democratic parties was ebbing away in Central and Northern Europe, giving way to pragmatic reformism save in Austria – until the fascist takeover in 1934 – and in Norway, where a lively Marxism led by a set of bright historians-cum-politicians suddenly flourished in and around a much radicalized Labour Party.

In France and in Britain, it took time for the new Marxist recruits to mature, helped neither by the continuingly vigorous non-Marxist traditions of the domestic labour and progressive movements nor by the sectarian instability of the new Communist parties. In Italy, Fascism soon forced Marxists into prison, exile or silence.

In Bolshevik Russia, Marxism blossomed, backed by generous academic endowments. Beginning in the early 1930s, however, Stalinist terrorist orthodoxy produced a prolonged stifling of creative thought. Well before that, the original authoritarian features of the revolution had constrained the intellectual debate, leading, for instance, Georges Gurvitch and Pitirim Sorokin to leave Russia to become prominent (non-Marxist) sociologists in Paris and Cambridge, Massachusetts, respectively.

In the rest of Eastern Europe, the prospects for Marxism darkened. Most of the successor states to the fallen multinational empires were or soon became authoritarian, with little tolerance of any form of Marxism or other radical thought, except for Czechoslovakia, which remained an increasingly beleaguered, nationalistically challenged left-of-centre democracy with a strong left-wing intellectual avant-garde, more aesthetic than theoretical. In any case, a pervasive nationalism marginalized Marxism among students and intellectuals.

EUROPEAN MARXISM AFTER THE SECOND WORLD WAR

The Second World War and its immediate aftermath changed the intellectual landscape of Europe. The new Communist regimes opened Eastern Europe to an institutionalization of Marxism, but under political regimes which furthered it neither as critical theory nor as science. A creative, abstract philosophical Marxism nevertheless developed from Yugoslavia to Poland, where it also managed, after the demise of Stalinism, to link up with sociology and class analysis in the works of Julian Hochfeld, Stefan Ossowski and others. In East Germany the economic historian Jürgen Kuczynski put together a monumental work of social history and statistics in forty volumes, *History of the Working Class under Capitalism.* But after 1968, most creative Marxism in Eastern Europe was silenced, exiled or abandoned.[68]

In Central and Northern Europe in the aftermath of the Second World War, there was an intellectual turn towards America. This was the time when American empirical social science, particularly sociology, political science and social psychology, were received and adopted in Europe, stimulated by generous American scholarships.[69] What caught on most easily were the more empiricist and conservative variants of US social science. Marxism was pushed

---

68. There were exceptions, such as the perceptive work on the trajectory of national movements by the Czech historian Miroslav Hroch.
69. Adorno, freshly returned from America, was also playing the empirical card in these years and was listened to as someone introducing empirical opinion research in West Germany. See R. Wiggershaus, *Die Frankfurter Schule*, Munich: Auflage, 1986, 501ff.

to the margins of far-left politics. In France and Italy, by contrast, Marxism reaped the fruits of the Resistance, also benefiting from the greater resilience of Latin high culture in the face of Americanization. Philosophy remained on its intellectual throne; among French and Italian intellectuals, Marxism, or a dialogue with Marxism, became the dominant mode of discourse. Large and resourceful Communist parties backed it up, and Marxism was also the theoretical language spoken in the socialist parties. In 1949 the writings of Antonio Gramsci were published, adding an original body of thought to the Marxist tradition, though for a long time only in Italy. Culture and intellectuals were thereby placed in the centre of analyses of politics and class power. Marxism guided postwar French historiography on the Revolution, academically consecrated by Georges Lefebvre's and Albert Soboul's successive incumbencies of the Sorbonne Chair on the History of the French Revolution. It was also pertinent to the great *Annales* school of historians.[70]

Britain, finally, had its own empirical traditions and so was not drawn into the American intellectual scene after the war. A significant Marxist current gradually emerged from Communist student politics of the late 1930s and early 1940s, preceded by a cohort of distinguished natural scientists, historians of science and ancient historians.[71] Britain's was the most important strand of empirical Marxism in Europe after the First World War. After 1945, its core was the Historians' Group of the Communist Party, which broke up in 1956. Before that, the group had successfully launched the scholarly journal *Past and Present*, which is still thriving. The postwar Marxist historians included Christopher Hill,

---

70. One of the best examples of a deep affinity with Marxism is the rather later work by Fernand Braudel, *Civilisation matérielle, economie et capitalisme: XVe–XVIIIe siècles*, 3 vols, Paris: Armand Colin, 1979.

71. J. D. Bernal, Gordon Childe, J. B. S. Haldane, Joseph Needham and others, crucially inspired by the visit of Boris Hessen and a Soviet delegation of historians of science in 1931.

Eric Hobsbawm and Edward Thompson, and in this milieu moved Raymond Williams, Maurice Dobb and George Thomson. While Isaac Deutscher had a different background and politics, as an historian and biographer of Trotsky and Stalin he fits well into the picture of British Marxism.[72]

While largely driven by it, social theory is not synchronized with political and social history. The late 1950s and the first half of the 1960s saw political Marxism in Western Europe at an ebb. The Austrian, West German and Swedish social-democratic parties divested their programmes of any Marxist traces in 1958–60. French socialism had discredited itself in the Algerian war and therewith its official Marxism. The Communist parties were ageing and isolated. The unexpected postwar boom was not merely continuing; it was accelerating. However, some of the most influential works of Western European Marxism appeared at this time: Louis Althusser's *For Marx* and *Reading 'Capital'* (1965), Isaac Deutscher's trilogy on Trotsky (1954–63), Jean-Paul Sartre's *Critique of Dialectical Reason* (1960), Edward Thompson's *The Making of the English Working Class* (1963).[73] The London-based *New Left Review*, which was to become the world's intellectually leading Marxist journal, was founded in 1960.[74]

---

72. See further R. Samuel, 'British Marxist Historians, 1880–1980: Part One', *New Left Review* 1: 120, March–April 1980, 21–96.

73. English-language editions of Althusser's cited works appeared in 1969 (*For Marx*) and 1970 (*Reading 'Capital'*), of Sartre's *Critique* in 1976.

74. The most important Italian Marxist journal, *Critica marxista*, issued by the Communist Party, began publication in 1962. The West German equivalents, *Neue Kritik, Das Argument, Prokla* and others, all came out of the student movement. In France the upheavals of 1968 did not change the landscape of established serious left-wing journals, none of which was very conducive to creative Marxist theory. *Les Temps Modernes*, founded by Sartre right after the war, was the intellectually dominant journal, but was in a literary-essay mould. So was the left-wing-Catholic *Esprit*. *La Pensée* was under tight Communist Party control. *L'Homme et la Société*, with roots in 1956 dissident Communism, was probably the journal most open to new Marxist thought.

The political situation then changed dramatically with the student revolt – an outcome of the new mass universities and the Vietnam War combined, and also inspired by China's 'Cultural Revolution'. At about the same time, the drying up of the labour markets paved the way for a resurgence of class conflict. The rapidly expanding subject of sociology provided the main academic battleground. Marxism became both the political language and the theoretical perspective for a generation of radicals who found in it the best way to understand the phenomena of colonial wars and underdevelopment, as well as the domestic socio-economic functioning of Western democracy. This neo-Marxism was a much larger wave than the original 'Western Marxism' but produced hardly anything as spectacular.

One reason for this was that politics and theory had become much more differentiated. Even the most brilliant and reflective political writings of this period are largely empirical. The theoretical and scholarly works, even of politically active people, are very academic. The best among the former genre are undoubtedly Régis Debray's writings on the revolutionary endeavours in Latin America.[75] Selecting the most impressive works of theory and scholarship from the neo-Marxist current in Europe is much more difficult and controversial. But Perry Anderson's monumental historical works, *Passages from Antiquity to Feudalism* and *Lineages of the Absolutist State* (both 1974), G.A. Cohen's *Karl Marx's Theory of History* (1978), and Nicos Poulantzas's *Political Power and Social Classes* (1968) will be on most people's short lists. They illustrate my argument very well.

---

75. R. Debray, *Révolution dans la révolution?*, Paris: Maspéro, 1967; and *La critique des armes*, Paris: Éditions du Seuil, 1974, 2 vols.

Neo-Marxism achieved Marx's inclusion in the classical canon of sociology and made Marxist or *marxisant* perspectives legitimate – albeit minority – views in most academic social science and humanities departments. Marxism entered anthropology primarily through the work of French anthropologists Maurice Godelier, Claude Meillassoux, Emmanuel Terray and others. And by linking up with the neo-Ricardian work of Gramsci's friend Piero Sraffa, economists mounted the first serious theoretical challenge to triumphant marginalism, pitting Cambridge, England – on the side of Ricardo and Marx – against Cambridge, Massachusetts.[76] But when the radical political thrust began to peter out in the second half of the 1970s, political Marxism evaporated rapidly. Academic Marxism also receded significantly, sometimes abandoned for more novel theoretical 'isms', sometimes submerged into ecumenical disciplinary practices. It has sustained itself best in sociology and historiography.

MARXISM IN THE NEW WORLDS

In the New Worlds created by early modern conquest and mass migration, the theoretical and practical struggle for modernity was largely external, against colonial Europe and by the colonized aliens against the colonists. Neither the internal conflict of historical forces nor the class formation of the forces in action were as important as they were in Europe.[77] The whole issue of the dialectics

---

76. M. Godelier, *Horizon, trajets marxistes en anthropologie*, Paris: F. Maspero, 1973; P. Sraffa, *Production of Commodities by Means of Commodities*, Cambridge: Cambridge University Press, 1960; G. Harcourt and N.F. Laing, eds, *Capital and Growth*, Harmondsworth: Penguin, 1971.
77. See further G. Therborn, 'The Right to Vote and the Four World Routes to/through Modernity', in *State Theory and State History*, ed. R. Torstendahl, London: Sage, 1992, 62–92; 'Routes to/through Modernity', in *Global Modernities*, M. Featherstone, S. Lash and R. Robertson, eds, London: Sage, 1995, 124–39.

of modernity, in particular its class dialectic, was less significant in the Americas and in Oceania. We should therefore expect Marxism to have played a much more modest role in the modern history of the New Worlds.

Marxist parties of any social significance arose as rare exceptions, and then late, only after the Second World War. Guyana, Chile and perhaps Cuba are the main ones. The Chicago publisher Charles H. Kerr became, around the turn of the century, a major intercontinental centre for the dissemination of Marxism in English, putting out, among other things, the first English translations of the second and third volumes of *Capital*. Immigrants spread Marxism to Latin America, where, for example, Argentina had a translation of *Capital* well before Sweden and Norway. Nevertheless, Marxism did not establish significant roots.

There was also a remarkable lack of creative individual contributions. Sidney Hook's *Toward the Understanding of Karl Marx* (1933) and Paul Sweezy's *The Theory of Capitalist Development* (1942) were solid and distinguished exegeses, but the only creatively original work of New-World Marxism in its first half-century or more was probably José Carlos Mariátegui's *Seven Essays of Interpretation of Peruvian Reality* (1928), a remarkable combination of radical European thought – including Pareto and Sorel – with a Leninist Marxism and Latin American cultural vanguardism applied to a whole spectrum of issues from economics to literature.[78]

However, after the Second World War, Marxist scholarship also underwent a tilt to the West, similar to that of science and scholarship in general, although in the

---

78. Mariátegui (1895–1930) was the founder of Peruvian Communism, a figure with many similarities to Gramsci, and in part inspired by the same intellectual ambience from a visit to Italy and Europe in 1919–23. It was with reference to his 'Shining Path' that Abimael Guzmán named his notorious guerilla movement Sendero Luminoso. See further M. Becker, *Mariátegui and Latin American Marxist Theory*, Athens, Ohio: Ohio University Press, 1993.

former case it took longer to mature. Marcuse was not given a very attractive offer to return to Germany, so he stayed in the US; apart from his later works, American Marxism received little from the anti-Fascist refugees. Paul Sweezy set up *Monthly Review* and the Monthly Review Press, which became the most important international platform for serious critiques of political economy. The new Marxist theory of the underdevelopment of capitalism came to centre around *MR*, in the works of Paul Baran (1957) and Andre Gunder Frank (1967), arguing that underdevelopment was not lack of development, but rather something which had developed out of global capitalism, as one constituent pole.[79] From Latin America in the mid-sixties came more sociologically oriented work on underdevelopment – above all, that of the Brazilian F. H. Cardoso[80] – often referred to as the dependency school, from its argument that Latin American underdevelopment depended on its relations to the metropoles of capitalism.

The late 1960s upheavals on the North American academic scene seem, on the whole, to have been more intellectually productive and innovative than parallel events in Europe or elsewhere. Highly creative contributions were suddenly made by a number of North American Marxists, the two most successful of whom are rivals. One is the historiographical work of Robert Brenner on the relevance of class struggle to the rise of modernity. Brenner's explicit and orthodox historical materialist perspective was asserted and sustained in a series of confrontations with other expert historians on the importance of class conflict to the emergence of industrial capitalist Europe, these being assembled under

79. P. A. Baran, *The Political Economy of Growth*, New York: Monthly Review Press, 1957; A.G. Frank, *Capitalism and Underdevelopment in Latin America*, New York: Monthly Review Press, 1967.
80. F. H. Cardoso and E. Faletto, *Dependência e desenvolvimento na América Latina*, Rio de Janeiro: Zahar, 1970.

the title *The Brenner Debate*.[81] More recently, Brenner has made yet another major contribution to a central issue of historiographical debate, this time arguing anew for the class character of the English Civil War.[82]

The other is Immanuel Wallerstein, whose sociologically informed works of scholarly synthesis may be more controversial than those of Brenner, but whose academic entrepreneurial acumen and achievements have had only one comparable Marxist parallel – Max Horkheimer.[83] In 1976, Wallerstein launched his project of 'world-systems analysis' – the examination of the largest conceivable social totality – around which he has built a research institute, a current within the American Sociological Association and a global network of collaborators. Wallerstein's dialectic of the capitalist world-system was explicitly directed against the then widespread evolutionary theory of the 'modernization' of separate societies.

This extraordinary creativity in North American Marxism also includes some very penetrating analyses of the labour process, again in conflict with each other (Braverman and Burawoy); the most ambitious analyses of class (Przeworski and Sprague, and Wright); and, aside from the work of Raymond Williams, the most innovative cultural inquiries (Jameson and many others, here unjustly but necessarily omitted).[84] Critical theory, then, has been received most warmly by left-wing academia in North

81. T. H. Aston and C. H. E. Philpin, eds, *The Brenner Debate*, Cambridge: Cambridge University Press, 1985.
82. R. Brenner, *Merchants and Revolution*, Princeton: Princeton University Press, 1993.
83. I. Wallerstein, *The Modern World System*, 3 vols, New York: Academic Press, 1976 onwards.
84. H. Braverman, *Labor and Monopoly Capital: The Degradation of Work in the Twentieth Century*, New York: Monthly Review Press, 1974; M. Burawoy, *Manufacturing Consent*, Chicago: University of Chicago Press, 1979, and *The Politics of Production*, London: Verso, 1985; A. Przeworski and J. Sprague, *Paper Stones. A History of Electoral Socialism*, Chicago: University of Chicago Press, 1986; E. O. Wright, *Classes*, London: Verso, 1985; F. Jameson, *Postmodernism, or, The Cultural Logic of Late Capitalism*, Durham: Duke University Press, 1991.

America. However, its best output has been about, rather than of, critical theory.[85] In this, the works of Martin Jay are exemplary.[86]

Modernity in the colonial zone has been particularly traumatic, with its fulcrum around the relationship of the conquered to the conquest and to the conqueror. Probably no one has captured the violent traumata involved better than Frantz Fanon, whose *The Wretched of the Earth* first appeared in 1961, with a preface by Sartre. It was the Comintern that made possible and propagated – through the Congress of Oppressed Peoples in Baku in November 1920, the formation of the Anti-Imperialist League, the global instigation of anticolonial Communist parties – a Marxist interpretation of colonialism and an anticolonialist identification with Marxism. But the outcome of all this was markedly more nationalists who used a Marxist vocabulary than actual Communists.[87] Marxism became the language of anticolonial movements and postcolonial powers, in Africa particularly, from the Algerian FLN to the Zimbabwean ZANU. But it was also very important on the Indian subcontinent – especially in secularized India – and in Indonesia, pushed very early by an extraordinary group of Dutch leftists led by Henricus Sneevliet.

Vietnam and French-ruled Indochina generally transformed a reception of French Marxism, culture and Communist political education into a variety of original forms, from phenomenological philosophy to the literally

---

85. The most creative American critical social theories have come from outside the Marxist tradition, such as A. Etzioni (*The Active Society*, New York: Collier-Macmillan, 1968 and *The Moral Dimension*, New York: Free Press, 1988) and R. Unger (*Politics: A Work in Constructive Social Theory*, 3 vols, Cambridge, Cambridge University Press, 1987).

86. M. Jay, *The Dialectical Imagination*, Boston: Little, Brown, 1973, and *Marxism and Totality*; see also S. E. Bronner, *Of Critical Theory and Its Theorists*, Cambridge: Blackwell Publishers, 1994.

87. See H. Carrère d'Encausse and S. Schram, eds, *Le marxisme et l'Asie 1853–1964*, Paris: Armand Colin, 1965; G. Padmore, *Pan-Africanism or Communism*, London: Dobson, 1956; C. Legum, *Pan-Africanism*, London: Pall Mall Press, 1962.

avuncular national Communism of Ho Chi Minh (Uncle Ho) and beyond to the sinister deliriums of Pol Pot. The *maoisant* turn of the French left-wing intelligentsia in the late 1960s burnt most of the remaining bridges between the mandarinates of Paris and Hanoi.

Korea had the unique experience of becoming a non-Western (Japanese) colony from as early as 1910. Here again, Western Marxism became the idiom of the anti-colonial movement which, with Soviet assistance, established a people's republic in the North, where Marxism became incorporated into a peculiar cult of the leader. The harsh class struggles and conflicts over democracy in the booming capitalist South have been conducive to fostering recent intellectual currents of Marxism, often of American academic inspiration, in the social sciences and in literary studies.

Black African culture, very distant from the Marxian dialectic of modernity, has not (yet) been able to sustain any significant Marxist intelligentsia. The most important Marxist intellectuals of Africa tend to be non-blacks, such as Samir Amin, an Egyptian Dakar-based development economist of world fame;[88] two East African class analysts of politics and law, Mahmood Mamdani and Issa Shivji, both of Indian descent; and the leadership of the South African Communist Party – which greatly influenced the ANC – who are mainly white. White South African academia has also included an embattled left-wing current from the late 1960s onwards.

In Indonesia, Marxism has been physically liquidated, both as an intellectual current and as a social force, in one of the most extensive political pogroms ever staged (in 1965–6). In Pakistan it has, on the whole, been out-ranked by Islam, in an anything but fair competition. India, on the other hand, has preserved a significant and sophisticated

---

88. S. Amin, *L'accumulation à l'échelle mondiale*, Paris: Éditions Anthropos, 1970.

Marxism, which originally entered the country from the US.[89] There is a tradition of high-level Marxist or *marxisant* economics, highlighted by the fact that the only non–North Atlantic economists included in the Cambridge–Cambridge controversy referred to above were two Italians and three Indians.[90] Above all, there is a lively and widespread historiographical tradition, including the mathematician-historian-polymath D.D. Kosambi, as well as Bipan Chandra, Irfan Habib, Harbans Mukhia[91] and the formidable group Subaltern Studies, directed by Ranajit Guha.[92] In Indian sociology, Marxism seems to have played a lesser role.[93]

China was never fully colonized and therefore largely travelled the fourth main road through modernity. The Japanese invasions of 1931 and 1937 did, however, put China under acute colonial threat, which gave rise to a highly original political Marxism in the 1940s, theoretically as well as practically under the leadership of Mao Zedong.

In the countries of externally induced modernization, we should expect Marxism to have led a marginal existence, kept at bay by the modernizing faction in power and largely alien to the populace dragged into modernity by the rulers. On the other hand, the opening to the importation of ideas should also have led to an early importation of Marxism and other radical ideas by whatever pro-modern factions are out of power. The relative significance of the two tendencies should depend on the amount of modernizing continuity and the amount of repression. The larger those two factors, the less Marxism there was.

---

89. G. Haupt and M. Reberioux, eds, *La Deuxième Internationale et l'Orient*, Paris: Cujas, 1967, p. 360.
90. Harcourt and Laing, *Capital and Growth*.
91. A. J. Syed, ed., *D. D. Kosambi on History and Society*, Bombay: University of Bombay, 1985; and Bipan Chandra, *Nationalism and Colonialism in Modern India*, New Delhi: Orient Longman, 1979.
92. R. Guha and G. C. Spivak, eds, *Selected Subaltern Studies*, Oxford: Oxford University Press, 1988.
93. T.K. Oommen and P.N. Mukherji, eds, *Indian Sociology*, Bombay: Popular Prakashan, 1986.

The former Ottoman Empire – Turkey, Iran and the Arab heartlands of Islam – and Sino-Japanese East Asia are the two major civilizations on this route to/through modernity. The former is on the continuist side of the spectrum and has never spawned any significant Marxism, theoretical or political. Japan, on the other hand, was more than merely the first relay of Marxism into Asia.[94] Its catastrophic defeat in 1945 opened the terrain to at least a socially significant middle-class Marxism centered around the Communist and socialist parties and the student movement. Theoretically, it has been characterized by a strong orthodox critique of political economy, spearheaded by the works of Kozo Uno and more recently expressed by Mishio Morishima, Makoto Itoh and others.[95]

The historical routes to and through modernity and their political dynamics have largely determined the trajectory of twentieth-century Marxism – not so much its substantial contents as its periods of expansion and contraction, allowing for the delayed impact of crucial generational events.

THE FUTURE OF DIALECTICS

As an interpretation, a critique, an analysis and, occasionally, a government of modernity, Marxism is without rival among modern conceptions of society, although the governmental record of politicians with Marxist claims is today widely regarded as full of failures. In intellectual terms, Marxism has maintained and developed itself primarily as historiography and, later, as sociology, as a socially mediated rather than an economically direct critique of political economy. But within the 'normal'

---

94. F. Andreucci, 'La diffusione e la volgarizzazione del marxismo', in E. Hobsbawn et al. eds, *Storia del marxisme*, vol. 2, Torino: Giulio Einaudi, 1979; cf. M. Silverberg, *Changing Song: The Marxist Manifestos of Nakano Shigeharo*, Princeton, NJ: Princeton University Press, 1990.
95. M. Itoh, *Value and Crisis: Essays on Marxian Economics in Japan*, New York: Monthly Review Press, 1980; M. Morishima, *Marx's Economics: A Dual Theory of Value and Growth*, Cambridge: Cambridge University Press, 1973.

pursuits of scholarship and science, all 'isms' are bound to disappear sooner or later. Its true philosophical *oeuvre*, from Max Adler to Louis Althusser and G. A. Cohen, has centred on understanding Marx and Marxism itself.[96] As such, it has been an in-house philosophy. Alternatively, with Henri Lefebvre and Jean-Paul Sartre, Marxist philosophy has been a proto-sociology.

Critical theory is only a Western moment of this global history, albeit a very important one, bringing out, perhaps more than any other variant, the problematic of Marxism as a dialectic of modernity. The conventional controversy of Marxism as a science or as a critique misses a decisive point. The scientific claims and self-confidence of Marxists, from Engels and Kautsky via the Austro-Marxists to Louis Althusser and his disciples, rested upon the assumption that the critique was, so to speak, already inherent in reality, in the actually existing labour movement. It was only when the latter could be written off that the crucial moment of antiscientific critique emerged.

At this juncture in history, after the exhaustion of the October Revolution and the decline of the industrial working class, the future relevance of the Marxian dialectic of modernity has to be thought anew. If there is anything valid in ideas about the processes of economic and cultural globalization, the division of humanity's saga into history and post-history makes no sense.[97] On the contrary, global interdependence and global chasms of misery and affluence are growing simultaneously. Polarizations of life chances,

---

96. True, they did address more general epistemological problems. Althusser (*Pour Marx*, Paris: François Maspero, 1965, back cover) originally presented the series, whose first items were *For Marx* and *Reading 'Capital'*, as intended 'to define and explore the field of a philosophy conceived as Theory of the production of knowledge'. But in fact there is a narrowing focus towards self-examination in Marxism and its dialectic, if we go from Adler (*Kausalität und Teleologie im Streit um die Wissenschaft*, Vienna 1904) to Adorno (*Negative Dialectics*), Althusser (*For Marx* and *Reading 'Capital'*) and Cohen (*Karl Marx's Theory of History: A Defence*, Oxford: Oxford University Press, 1978).
97. F. Fukuyama, *The End of History*, New York: Penguin, 1992.

if not of rival powers, are building in the developed metropoles. A dialectical understanding of this unity of opposites is called for today, hardly less than at the time of Karl Marx. This is a new moment of critique, lacking the scientific backdrop of class as well as the apocalyptics of Korsch and Lukács, and requiring a human commitment beyond the academic division of labour. But again, *pace* Habermas, a critique of prevailing economics seems to be called for more urgently than a theory of communicative action.

Since neither capitalism nor its polarizations of life courses appear very likely to disappear in the foreseeable future, there is a good chance that the spectre of Marx will continue to haunt social thought.[98] The most obvious way forward for social theorizing inspired by Marx will be to look at what is currently happening to the venerable couplet of the forces and relations of production on a global scale and their conflictual effects on social relations. Marxism may no longer have any solutions ready to hand, but its critical edge is not necessarily blunted.

Finally, with the return of socialism from science to utopia, there is a good chance that men and women concerned with critical social thought will turn with increasing interest to the great philosopher-historian of hope, Ernst Bloch, who pointed out that 'Marxism, in all its analyses the coldest detective, takes the fairy-tale seriously, takes the dream of a Golden Age practically.'[99] The free society without exploitation and alienation which the critical dialecticians hoped for, sometimes against all odds, is perhaps not so much a failure of the past as something that has not yet come to pass.

---

98. See J. Derrida, *Spectres de Marx*, Paris: Galilée, 1993.
99. E. Bloch, *The Principle of Hope* (1959), trans. N. Plaice, S. Plaice and P. Knight, Oxford: Basil Blackwell Ltd, 1986, vol. 3, 1370, emphasis omitted.

3

After Dialectics:
Radical Social Theory in the
North at the Dawn of
the Twenty-first Century

If socialism and liberalism have both been central to modern political and social thought, then during the twentieth century it was socialism, in a loose ecumenical sense, that was the more successful of the two in terms of intellectual attraction and public support.[1] Socialism was emblazoned on the banners of mass parties in Brazil, Britain, China, France, Germany, India, Indonesia, Italy, Japan, Mexico, Russia, South Africa – in fact, virtually every major country of the globe, with the exception of Nigeria and the US. It was embraced at least as a rhetorical goal by a range of locally powerful parties from Arctic social democrats to African nationalists. Socialism and Communism exercised

---

1. This text grew from an initial invitation to contribute to a collection on different aspects of European social theory, focusing on the question of 'Post-Marxism and the Left', and was later expanded for *New Left Review*. Any survey of a field as broad as this will be liable to omissions and oversights, as well as to the political, personal and generational inclinations of its author.

a powerful attraction over some of the most brilliant minds of the last century: Einstein was a socialist, who wrote a manifesto entitled 'Why Socialism?' for the founding issue of the US Marxist journal *Monthly Review*; Picasso was a Communist, who designed the logo of post-Second World War Communist-led peace movements. In spite of its conservatively defined original task and its own staunchly conservative traditions, the Swedish Academy has allotted the Nobel Prize for literature to a series of left-wing writers, from Romain Rolland to Elfriede Jelinek.

In the 1960s and 1970s, following two springtides in the aftermaths of the twentieth century's two world wars, varieties of socialism reached their maximum influence and transformational ambition, as did socialism's central, if not its sole, theoretical canon: Marxism. Geopolitically, the Soviet Union attained parity with the US, which was defeated by the Vietnamese Communists. The Chinese Cultural Revolution was the largest attempt at radical social change ever carried out, and was seen as a dazzling red beacon by many people all over the world. Africa north of the Limpopo was swept by decolonization and embarked on projects of socialist nation-building. In Latin America the Cuban Revolution inspired a hemispheric surge of revolutionary socialist politics, followed by another example, different but allied, in Chile.

Trade-union movements in the most developed countries reached their highest levels of affiliation in the mid-1970s. In Western Europe and the oceanic antipodes, social democracy was marching forward, both electorally and in its reform programme. In Sweden from 1968 to 1976, and in France between 1978 and 1981, social democrats presented their most radical concrete plans ever for social change. Militant working-class movements of strikes, demonstrations and workplace occupations shook France in May 1968 and Italy in the autumn of 1969. Student movements, which in Europe had historically been mainly right-wing, emerged as powerful leftist forces across Europe, the Americas, large parts of Africa from South Africa to Ethiopia and, in less pronounced forms, the Arab North, Asia from Istanbul to Bangkok and Tokyo, and Oceania. Marx and Marxism pushed open the doors to the academy in some of the major capitalist countries, achieving a strong influence there, even if they were never hegemonic in any significant intellectual centre outside Italy and France.

Then, suddenly, the high water withdrew and was followed by a neoliberal tsunami. Socialist constructions were knocked down, many of them proving ramshackle or fake in the process; socialist ideas and Marxist theories were engulfed in the deluge. Privatization became the global order of the day, formulated in the Washington Consensus of the US Treasury, the IMF and the World Bank. At the dawn of the twenty-first century, not only liberal capitalism but also empire and imperialism have staged a triumphant return, and with them the world-views of the Belle Epoque. The explanation of this sudden turn, and why it happened in the last two decades of the twentieth century, is a task far beyond the scope of this brief overview of the landscape of Left social theory after the neoliberal 'disaster'. Some outline, however, must be given of the changing parameters within which such theorization has taken place, before a summary picture of responses can be provided.

THE TURN OF MODERNITY

Whether its analysis tends towards celebration and acceptance or towards critique and rejection, social theorization depends on the social world it theorizes. A major reason for studying the present is to understand the power it exercises, and critiques of it are largely, if not absolutely, dependent on the hope of a possible different world. Such hope, in turn, depends on the visibility, however faint, of some alternative power or force with the potential to carry the critique forward into active change. What happened to socialism and Marxism in the 1980s and 1990s was that the alternative forces appeared to melt away. While the inequalities of capitalism were increasing in most countries, while the global gap between rich and poor was widening, and while the brutality of the rulers of the main capitalist states was reaffirmed again and again, the dialectic of capitalism was imploding. Capital's new push was accompanied not by any strengthening of the working-class and anticapitalist movements, nor by the opening of a systemic exit into another mode of production – at least not from a perspective visible to the naked eye. On the contrary, labour was weakened and embryonic systemic alternatives either fell apart or were completely marginalized. The global confluence of left-wing political defeats and social meltdowns in the last two decades of the twentieth century was, by any measure, overwhelming.

Any analytical assessment, however, has to take into account the slow work of time. The ideas of most contemporary theorists were actually formed during earlier conjunctions of hope and power. Existing theory still mainly registers the response of this preceding generation to the turn of the 1980s and 1990s; at the same time, a new layer of leftists is emerging from the World Social Forums, the antiglobalization movement and the Indo-American mobilizations from Chiapas to Bolivia and beyond. Meanwhile, the sociopolitical meaning of the new Muslim anti-imperialism is yet to be determined.

In the rich capitalist countries, the structural turn to deindustrialization and the mishandling by the centre-left of the difficult conjuncture of mass unemployment and soaring inflation during the 1970s prepared the way for the revenge of neoliberalism, spearheaded in industrialization's country of origin. When the new economic doctrine turned out to be an unexpectedly aggressive challenge, the main powers that were supposedly 'building socialism' adopted different strategies. That of the Soviet

Union would prove suicidal: trying to placate political liberalism while letting the economy spiral downwards by tolerating increasingly aggressive barracuda bites. The Chinese, and later the Vietnamese, took the 'free-market' road: if capitalism is the only show on earth, we are going to run it. After the failures and moral hollowness of the Chinese Cultural Revolution, the Chinese Communist Party – for all its former Maoist diatribes against 'capitalist roaders' – was the political force that was most committed to following that route.

In Latin America, both reformist and revolutionary hopes had been quenched in blood by the end of the 1970s. In the Arab world, the successful Israeli attack in 1967 had shattered the secular Left. African client states of Cold War Communism turned their coats with the disappearance of their patrons. The huge Indonesian Communist Party had literally been massacred in 1965. Chilean Marxism, both socialist and Communist, never recovered from the blow of 1973. In Europe, the PCI has dissolved itself, and the PCF has shrunk to the size of a large sect. But West Bengal, an Indian state with a population the size of Germany's, has continued to re-elect its Communist government, and a Caribbean Castroism has managed to survive, revivified by recent developments in Venezuela and Bolivia. Red banners are still kept flying by sizeable minorities in southern Europe, from Portugal to Greece, and by the largest party of Greek Cyprus, the moderate AKEL. Perhaps with the exception of the latter, however, these are parties of testimony rather than of hope. The social-democratic aspirations of post-Communist Europe have come to little; its parties have tended to be either liberal, corrupt or both. Socialist hopes of post-apartheid South Africa have also come to nothing, although the ANC does provide an example of working democracy in Africa. The left-wing turn of Latin American countries in the 2000s owes little to classical socialist or Marxist thought, deriving more inspiration from radical Catholicism in the case of Brazil, from Latin American populism in Argentina and Venezuela and from indigenous peoples' mobilization in Bolivia – although the Movement to Socialism of President Evo Morales was largely built by former cadres from the left-wing miners' union. Nevertheless, in each, and particularly in the Bolivian case, there is an articulate left-wing socialist component.

The world has not yet been made entirely safe for liberalism. New radical forces continue to emerge: populist movements in Indo-America, waves of migration throwing up immigrants' movements in the 'First World', and a whole gamut of political manifestations of Islam, from Islamist democracy to sectarian terrorism. The most interesting of these, crucial for coming developments, may be the advent of a social Islamism, comparable to the social Catholicism of Europe from the Netherlands to Austria a century ago. But the old cartography of 'roads to socialism' has lost its bearings. New compasses of the Left have to be made; it should be expected that this will take some time.

Marxism's Broken Triangle

As a minimum framework for situating recent turns of left-wing social theory, we need to look at how Marxist and socialist thought has been embedded in cultural history. This entails, first, a look at the specific construction of Marxism as an 'ism' and at the forces bearing upon that structure. Secondly, Marxism and socialism should be recognized as parts of a wider cultural ensemble, that of modernity, and therefore affected by the vicissitudes of the latter.

The history of Marxism may best be seen as a triangulation, growing out of both the historical situation and the extraordinary range of interests of its founding fathers. The 'ism' has three different poles, of varying distances from each other, not to mention varying pole-coalitions. Intellectually, Marxism was first of all a historical social science, in the broad Germanic sense of *Wissenschaft*, focused on the operation of capitalism and, more generally, on historical developments determined 'in the last instance' by the dynamics of the forces and relations of production. Secondly, it was a philosophy of contradictions or dialectics, with epistemological and ontological ambitions, no less than ethical implications. Thirdly, Marxism was a mode of politics of a socialist, working-class kind, providing a compass and a road-map to the revolutionary overthrow of the existing order. The politics was the overdetermining apex of the triangle, making the 'ism' a social current, not just an intellectual lineage. Historical materialism, with the Marxian critique of political economy, and materialist dialectics, with the social philosophy of alienation and commodity fetishism, had their intrinsic intellectual attractions, but these were usually connected to sympathies with, and often commitment to, a socialist class politics. In Marx-*ism*, the relation of politics to science, historiography and philosophy were always asymmetrical. If and when political leadership was differentiated from theoretical leadership, it was always political power which gained the upper hand, although political leadership during the first two generations after Marx usually required a capacity for theoretical argumentation.

Marx, Engels, Kautsky – the chief theoretician of the social-democratic Second International – and Lenin, each in his own way, mastered all three genres. Stalin and Mao, too, dabbled in all three. However impressive the intellectual-cum-political versatility and expertise of these founding generations, such qualities were also an expression of the early modernity of the late nineteenth century, when intellectual discourse had as yet scarcely been subdivided into separate disciplines, and of the natural preponderance of politics. In the course of the twentieth century, the length of the sides of the triangle would be increasingly extended. Any serious attempt at understanding 'post-Marxism' will have to deal with this triangle of social science, politics and philosophy.

The Marxism that emerged in Western Europe after the First World War was basically philosophical in approach; originally eschatologically connected to revolutionary politics (Lukács, Korsch, Gramsci), it later either stood discreetly aloof from it (the Frankfurt School) or was only indirectly related to it (Althusser, Lefebvre, Sartre), even if its exponents were linked by party membership, as in the first two cases.[2] In spite of the hard sociological lessons of the Frankfurters in US exile, and of the scientific thrust of the Althusserians, European Marxist philosophers in this period hardly ever engaged intellectually with Marxist social scientists or historians.

A Marxist mode of politics never attracted enough support to become consolidated in Western Europe as a distinctive political practice. It was always open to opportunistic enterprise and to authoritarian legitimation. This made what perhaps may be called the 'natural' Marxist coalition of politics and social science difficult and rare. There was, of course, one important link: the political commitment to socialism, in the historical sense of a different kind of society. In the 1960s, 1970s, even in the early 1980s, this was a commitment not only of radical intellectuals and youthful revolutionaries. It was professed by mass parties or by significant currents within them, such as the British Labour Party and continental Western European social democracies. There was also the 'actually existing' fact that a sizeable group of states, two of them very powerful, were 'building socialism'. Belief in their achievement was limited, but the view that they at least constituted an ongoing social construction site – even if temporarily stagnant or perhaps decaying – was widespread.

Socialist politics, in the ambiguous senses referred to,

2. See P. Anderson, *Considerations on Western Marxism*, London: New Left Books, 1976.

kept the Marxist triangle together, even if there was little in it of specifically Marxist intent. But socialist politics disintegrated in the course of the 1980s: bogged down and driven to surrender in France; electorally crushed in Britain and pushed onto the defensive in Scandinavia; abruptly turning rightwards for geopolitical and other reasons in Southern Europe; abandoned or fatally undermined in Communist Eurasia; already crushed under the militarist boot in Latin America. This pulled the carpet from under Marxism as a social science, its analyses losing any discernible potential audience. Marxist philosophy, like historiography and social science, came to rely on academic appointments. Perhaps because it was immune to empirical disproof, philosophy managed better, maintaining a link to marginal revolutionary politics, especially in parts of Latin Europe.

The Marxist triangle of social science, politics and philosophy has been broken – in all likelihood, irremediably. This is not to say that socialist politics, premised on claims for a different, socialist society, have disappeared. Where the electoral system allows its expression, support for such a politics oscillates between 5 and 20 per cent of the national vote, but it could grow. Political ideologies and orientations have their ups and downs, and postsocialism may soon be overshadowed by some new socialism. But the underdevelopment of Marxist political theory, together with the social restructuring of capitalist societies, makes it unlikely that an ascendant socialist politics would be very Marxist. The zenith of the industrial working class has passed, while many previously neglected political subjects are coming to the fore.

Under non-repressive conditions, Marx-*ism* is unlikely to exercise an attraction as social science or historiography for post-1990s cohorts of committed socialist scholars. By the standards of physics or biology, the advances of social science and historical scholarship may look modest; they nevertheless represent enormous strides forward since the age of *Das Kapital*. Yet, as we have previously noted, since each generation of social scientists tends to find fresh sources of inspiration among the classics of social thought, it seems most likely that Marx will be rediscovered many times over in the future; novel interpretations will be made and new insights found – though conducive to little *ism*-ish identification. Philosophers, on the other hand, are habitually, rather than occasionally, bent over their predecessors. Whether Marx will achieve the 2,500-year longevity of Plato, Aristotle and Confucius is an open question, but the possibility cannot be ruled out. A ghost never dies, as Derrida said.[3] The history of philosophy tends ever to generate new techniques of reading.

Challenge of Postmodernism

Left and Marxist social theory must also be situated within the broader cultural framework of modernity within which it was first articulated, and by whose vicissitudes it will inevitably be affected. Just such a framework appeared around 1980 in the challenge of postmodernism. While postmodernism derived from the arts and from cultural philosophy, it has also claimed to speak about society, about culture in an anthropological sense and about history and the current historical situation of humankind. There is, then, an area of encounter and contest with contemporary historiography and social science. What might be the contribution from an analytical perspective of historiography and empirical sociology?

Obviously, there is no single correct definition of modernity and the modern. But the most fruitful definitions of concepts taken from general language tend to be the least arbitrary and idiosyncratic ones, which usually implies a respect for etymological meaning and an abstention from

---

3. J. Derrida, *Spectres de Marx*, Paris: Galilée, 1993, 163.

loading the definition with a priori connotations. Modernity
should thus be seen as a temporal orientation only. Modernity is a culture claiming to be modern, in the sense of
turning its back on the past – the old, the traditional, the
passé – and looking into the future as a reachable, novel
horizon. Modern man/woman, society, civilization have a
direction: 'forward', or, as it was phrased in the old GDR
and in post-independence Ghana, 'Forward ever, back-
wards never'.[4] Rather than trivializing the concept of
modernity by attempting to translate it into a set of concrete
institutions, whether of capitalism or politics, or into a
particular conception of rationality or agency so that it can
more easily be philosophically targeted, it is more useful
to deploy it solely as a temporal signifier, in order to allow
it to retain its analytical edge.

What would be the use of modernity – the German
Moderne – in this sense? Why not follow Jameson's advice
of 'substituting capitalism for modernity'?[5] Modernity is
useful to many because of its broader, extra-economic
connotations. A cultural history of, say, *Berliner Moderne*
is hardly synonymous with a history of capitalism in
Berlin, and not necessarily of illegitimate interest.[6]
Modernity directs attention to important semantic shifts,
otherwise easily neglected. Take the word 'revolution',
for example. As a premodern concept it pointed back-
wards, 'rolling back', or to recurrent cyclical motions,

---

4. See R. Koselleck, *Vergangene Zukunft*, Frankfurt: Suhrkamp, 1979, 314ff; J.
Habermas, *Der philosophische Diskurs der Moderne*, Frankfurt, Suhrkamp, 1985,
14–15.
5. F. Jameson, *A Singular Modernity*, 215.
6. Nor should social modernism be equated with the postwar social theory of
'modernization', as Jeffrey Alexander proposed some years ago. Modernization
was a particular sociocultural theory of historical evolution, attacked by Wallerstein
and others not from an 'antimodern' position, but for its methodological nationalism
and its rosy-idealist evolutionism, looking away from capitalism, exploitation,
colonialism and 'the development of underdevelopment'. See J. Alexander,
'Modern, Anti, Post, Neo', *New Left Review* 1: 210, March–April 2005.

as in Copernicus's *On the Revolutions of the Heavenly Spheres* or the French Enlightenment *Encyclopédie*, in which the main entry refers to clocks and clock-making. Only after 1789 did 'revolution' become a door to the future, as did, a little later, another 're-' term: 'reform'.

As a historical concept, modernity also requires us to distinguish and analyze different routes towards it, with their enduring, if not unalterable, consequences. As was explored in the preceding chapter, four major roads to and through modernity may be discerned: the European one of civil war and internal conflict; the New World path of settlement, with its external premodern Others – both the corrupt country of origin and the local natives; the traumatic road of colonial conquest and anticolonial nationalism; and the 'reactive modernization' from above, pioneered by Japan. Finally, a time concept of modernity is also a way of grasping the significance of postmodernity, as a questioning of, or a loss of belief in, the future narratives of the modern. Insofar as 'forward' and 'backward', progressive and reactionary, have lost all meaning, we have entered a postmodern world.

Marx and Marxism were quite modern in this sense, invoking the term again and again in *The Communist Manifesto* and *Capital*, the 'ultimate purpose of which' was to 'disclose the economic law of motion of modern society', as Marx put it in his preface to the first edition of volume one.[7] However, and this was crucial, it was a *dialectical* conception of modernity, seen as inherently contradictory. The modernity of capitalism and of the bourgeoisie were hailed, but at the same time attacked as exploitative and alienating. This dialectical understanding of modernity was, in a sense, the very core of Marxian thought. It affirmed the progressive nature of capitalism, of the bourgeoisie, even of capitalist imperialist rule (in ways

---

7. See M. Berman, *All That Is Solid Melts Into Air*, London: Verso, 1983.

that many would now find insensitive to the victims of colonialism), while at the same time not only denouncing them but also organizing the resistance against them. In broad cultural-historical terms, Marxism may be seen as Her Majesty Modernity's Loyal Opposition.[8] But if Marxism in this core cultural sense (as well as the recent challenges to it) can only be understood in terms of its dialectical conception of modernity, this latter also needs to be located in contradistinction to other important 'master narratives of modernity'. The most influential of these might be summarized as follows:

Table 3.1: Master Narratives of Modernity

THE PAST:	THE FUTURE:
Ignorance, superstition, subservience	Emancipation: rational, individual enlightenment
Oppression, unfreedom	Emancipation/liberation: collective
Poverty, disease, stagnation	Growth, progress, development
Conditions of no/less competition	Survival of the fittest
Rule-bound, imitative	Creative vitality

Let us take the points in Table 3.1 in order. Firstly, if the Kantian notion of rational enlightenment has lost much of its appeal by the early twenty-first century, it should be recognized that it remains at the centre of such important controversies as, for example, how to explain, prevent and cope with HIV/AIDS and other lethal diseases in Africa and other parts of the world. Is witchcraft a major source of sickness and death? Is penetration of a virgin a cure for AIDS?

Secondly, the concept of collective emancipation or

---

8. See Chapter 2 in this volume.

liberation has undergone a remarkable mutation over the past few decades as part of the process of postmodernization. It has largely lost its former social referents – the working class, the colonized, women, gays and lesbians – and, above all, its earlier socialist horizons of emancipation from capitalism. But it has not disappeared. It re-emerges today in militant liberal-democratic discourse, itself a form of right-wing modernism, where it now refers to liberation from a select group of 'anti-Western' authoritarian regimes: Communist, post-Communist, or Muslim and Arab. In Indo-Latin America, on the other hand, emancipation has acquired a new social urgency as indigenous populations raise demands for a more equitable division of resources.

Thirdly, horizons of growth and progress still govern the expectations of all modern economies, erstwhile 'constructions of socialism' as well as every variety of capitalism, including the reigning neoliberalism. Growth and progress also constitute the continuing story that science tells of itself and form the creed of all contemporary academic authorities.

Fourthly, the survival of the fittest and social Darwinism have been given a new impetus by neoliberal globalization, after their postfascist quarantine. According to this view, only the fittest and the meanest will deserve to survive the free-for-all of global competition. Fifth and finally, the collapse of rule-bound artistic academicism has left artistic modernism without a target, other than older modernists. The modern conflict between the avant-garde and tradition has been replaced by a succession of fashions.

Marx harboured all the above modern perspectives, although collective human emancipation and economic development were most central to him. However, what distinguished Marx and Marxism from other strands of modernist thought was a focus on the contradictory character of the modern era, and on these contradictions and conflicts as its most important dynamics.

Against the linear liberal projects of individualization,

Table 3.2: Marxian Dialectics of Capitalist Modernity

ADVANCE:	CONTRADICTION/CONFLICT:
Individualization	Atomization, alienation
Productivity development	Exploitation and distributive polarization
	Outgrowing existing relations of production
Capitalist extension	Proletarian unification and strengthening
Globalization	Anti-imperialist revolts

rationalization and growth as the bases for 'modernization', Marxism set a dialectical perspective of emancipation – explicitly affirming that capitalism and colonialism were forms of exploitation as well as of progress, as can be seen in Table 3.2. The Marxist perspective also differed from the Weberian notion of the rationalization of markets and bureaucracies as an 'iron cage'. The contradictions of modernity, according to Marx, were harbingers of radical change. The labour movement in capitalist countries, the socialist-feminist movement, the anticolonial liberation movements and 'actually existing' socialist countries, whatever their faults, were seen as carriers of a different future, of a modernist project of emancipation. By the 1990s, however, that belief in the future had been fundamentally shattered.

Postmodernism attacked all the grand narratives of modernity, while usually ignoring the dialectical conception of Marxism. But all its sociopolitical advances, all its conquests of ideological space, were against the modernist Left. At the same time, right-wing modernism defeated almost all its traditionalist conservative rivals, most successfully in Thatcher's Britain – for neoliberalism may be seen as a high modernism of the Right and, as noted, it has scarcely been dented by postmodernist arguments.

The reinvigorated American Right is a vivid illustration of the current entanglements of modernity.[9] While the American Right recruits its storm troopers from Christian fundamentalists, its hegemonic tenor arises from its 'willingness to embrace the future', which it sees as belonging to itself.[10] (The theological celebration of worldly success by mainstream Christian evangelicalism facilitates, of course, this powerful brew of secular modernism and religious fundamentalism.) Significantly, while the Left's commitment to social revolution has been silenced or muted, the American Right is trumpeting 'regime change'.

Modernity has not been abandoned as an intellectual position. It has been defended by theorists both from the 'Third Way' and from the old Far Left.[11] In a well-funded research and publishing programme at the German publisher Suhrkamp Verlag, Ulrich Beck has gone so far as to proclaim a 'second modernity'. But the sociopolitical challenge across the whole Left–Right spectrum has scarcely begun to be confronted. In fact, Beck's *Risk Society*, first published in Germany in 1986 and a major theoretical work of recent decades, did provide a possible basis for a new conception of modernity: 'Risk may be defined as a systematic way of dealing with hazards and insecurities induced and introduced by modernization itself. Risks . . . are politically reflexive.'[12] This is an important societal conceptualization – risk being a key concept of economics – that also found a political resonance in environmental circles. However, its critical edge is blunted by two features: first, its basic blindness to what

---

10. J. Micklethwait and A. Wooldridge, *The Right Nation*, London, Penguin, 2004, 346ff.
11. See for example J. Habermas, *Der philosophische Diskurs der Moderne*; A. Callinicos, *Against Postmodernism*, Cambridge: Palgrave Macmillan, 1989; U. Beck, A. Giddens and S. Lash, *Reflexive Modernization*, Cambridge: Polity, 1994; T. Eagleton, *The Illusions of Postmodernism*, Oxford: WileyBlackwell, 1996.
12. U. Beck, *Risk Society*, London: Sage Publications, 1992, 21, italics omitted.

was happening rightwards of the centre on the political scale, the aforementioned rise of right-wing liberal modernism – initially less strong in Germany than in the Anglo-Saxon world, but politically triumphant well before its enthronement in the most recent *Grosse Koalition*. Second, the specific institutional content of Beck's 'new', later 'second', modernity – the demise of class, full employment and the nation-state; the 'release' of individuals from industrial institutions – lays his perceptive grasp of a changed time-frame open to charges of arbitrary selectivity, empirical unreliability, or both.

Postmodernist discourse has something important to teach, but it should be subjected to a symptomatic rather than a literal reading, as a questioning of non-dialectical conceptions of modernity, as a symptom of the disorientation of the (ex-)Left, and as a form of myopia towards the world beyond the North Atlantic. The postmodernization of the world remains very uneven. At the frenzied pace of aesthetic discourse, postmodernism may even be 'over', as one of its former publicists put it in a second-edition epilogue.[13] In 2002 Jameson noted the end of the post-modern 'general agreement', and 'in the last few years . . . the return to and the re-establishment of all kinds of old things'.[14] Bauman, in advanced age still tuned to the shift-ing sirens of the times, has turned to peddling 'liquid modernity' instead of postmodernity.[15] Nevertheless, the two decades of postmodernism, the 1980s and 1990s, produced a rift in cultural social thought, itself a symptom of the politico-economic times, which has not been over-come. The future as novelty, as difference, disappeared behind a smokescreen.

---

13. Hutcheon, *The Politics of Postmodernism*, 166.
14. Jameson, *A Singular Modernity*, 1.
15. Z. Bauman, *Liquid Modernity*, Cambridge: Polity, 2000.

While ecological and feminist critiques of modernist visions of growth, development and progress have become significant side-currents in the centres of capitalism – often incorporated, in diluted forms, into the mainstream of enlightened liberalism – Third World critiques of what we may call, with a respectful bow to the Peruvian social theorist Anibal Quijano, the coloniality of modernity, or the coloniality of anticolonial nationalism, have hardly penetrated the walls of North Atlantic social theory. This has always been an important theme in Indian thought, if usually in a somewhat uneasy alliance with modernist nationalism, exemplified in the cooperation between Gandhi and Nehru. At the Mumbai Social Forum in 2004, a main-stage banner proclaimed 'People Do Not Want Development, They Just Want to Live'. This made some sense to the many recent Indian social movements pitting local, often 'tribal' people and ecologists against modern dam and other developmentalist projects. Seen alongside the terrible Mumbai slums, however, the attack on developmentalism appears less convincing.

However, in a country like Bolivia, the coloniality of modernity is more palpable, evidenced in the country's long post-independence history of racist politics and projects of economic and cultural 'modernization' that left the indigenous majority out in the cold and poverty of the *altiplano*. The platform of the current elected leadership of Bolivia, President Evo Morales and Vice-President Álvaro García Linera, is neither traditionalist, modernist nor post-modernist. Intellectually as well as politically impressive, it is a bold attempt at clearing a path to an alternative modernity, blazing a new trail for Marxism in the Andes.

In summary, we may say that modernity turned at the end of the twentieth century, but in several directions: to the right; into postmodernism; and into theoretical and political searches for new modernities.

Definitions

Now that the broader political and cultural-intellectual parameters of recent social theorizing have been laid out, there remains a further preliminary question to be asked before we can consider the current shape of the field: What is social theory? The definition deployed here sees social theory as strung between two ambitious poles: on the one hand, providing a comprehensive explanatory framework for a set of social phenomena; on the other, 'making sense of' such phenomena. In other words, this is an ecumenical conception of 'theory' that applies both to explanation – the more wide-ranging, the more important – and to *Sinnstiftung*, the constitution of meaning.

In terms of the 'sense-making' pole, the later salience of philosophy in the classical Marxist triangle of social science, philosophy and politics, and the former's far greater resilience to empirical developments, mean that the contributions of political and social philosophy are of particular importance to an overview of recent social theory emanating from the Left. In terms of the second pole, that of empirical social science, it should perhaps be reiterated that theory is not a separate field or a subdiscipline, a form of research-free armchair thinking, but the guiding compass of empirical investigation. It was in these terms that Pierre Bourdieu, for instance, criticized current Anglo-Saxon conceptions of social theory.[16] Attention will also be given to that kind of theory in scientific action.

It should be underlined at the outset that what follows is by no means a general survey of the intellectual production of the contemporary Left. A strict definition of social theory, centred on the present, must exclude the work of historians and scholars of intellectual history, and thereby some of the most gifted minds of the international Left. Another fruitful area for the Left during recent years has

---

16. See P. Bourdieu, *Réponses*, Paris: Seuil, 1992, 86, 136ff.

been that of geopolitics and interstate relations, yielding important new work on imperialism and imperial power; but again, this involves little social theorizing as such.[17]

However, the fact that in 2004 the British Academy organized an official conference titled 'Marxist Historiography: Alive, Dead or Moribund?' was a significant theoretical event. The answer that clearly resonated was 'Alive!', with the qualification that what was alive was Marx 'the diagnostician' and not the 'prophet', as the academy's president put it in his introduction. The editor of the ensuing volume, the great Oxford medieval historian Chris Wickham, summed up his own field by saying that 'in medieval economic and social history, far from Marxist ideas being dead or moribund, they are everywhere'.

The challenges to left-wing social thought posed by postmodernity and by the neomodern Right have been met in very different ways. Disregarding cases of actual flight from radical thought, which fall outside the scope of this article, I will first track new thematics in the responses of left-of-centre scholars, and then attempt to locate some of the general shifts in their theoretico-political positionings. Since restrictions of space permit neither lengthy expositions nor elaborate analyses of these variations, I have opted for a regional road-map, mainly restricted to Western Europe and North America.

MODES OF THE LEFT'S RESPONSE

Europe's Theological Turn

The most surprising theoretical development in left-wing social philosophy in the past decade has been a new

---

17. The yearbook *Socialist Register* has been a central focus in this field, publishing work by, among others, Aijaz Ahmad, Noam Chomsky, Sam Gindin, Peter Gowan, David Harvey, Colin Leys, Leo Panitch, John Saul, Bob Sutcliffe and Ellen Wood.

theological turn. In the main, this has not meant an embrace of religious faith, although some former left-wing intellectuals have come to affirm an ethnoreligious Jewishness, and there is often an indication of a particular personal relation, beyond belief, to religion or to a religious figure – as when Régis Debray writes: 'Three things have occupied my life [as a thinker], war, art and religion.'[18] Rather, the theological turn has manifested itself in a scholarly interest in religion and in a use of religious examples in philosophical and political argumentation. In contrast to the Latin American theology of liberation, which was a religious commitment to social justice led by ordained Catholic priests, the European form is a theology of discourse.

The principal work here is that of Debray who, in *Le feu sacré* (2003) and *God: An Itinerary* (2004), has turned his literary talents to original scholarly investigations into the structures of the Judeo-Christian narratives, the religious 'procedures of memorization, displacement and organization', and the re-lit fires of religion around the world.[19] Debray, however, had first developed these themes in his *Critique of Political Reason* (1981/1983), considerations on the religious unconscious in politics and political forms of the sacred; in fact, he began his adult religious studies with a biography of the eleventh-century Pope Gregory, a work he read while imprisoned as a revolutionary in the small Bolivian town of Camiri, where Christian texts were the only uncensored reading matter.[20]

Alain Badiou, a former Maoist and still an active far-left militant as well as a philosopher, refers to an old, poetic and personal relationship to Saint Paul, to whom he turns in his 'search for a new militant figure . . . called upon to succeed the one installed by Lenin'. Badiou's

18. R. Debray, *Le feu sacré*, Paris: Fayard, 2003.
19. R. Debray, *God: An Itinerary*, London: Verso, 2004.
20. R. Debray, *Critique of Political Reason*, London: Verso, 1983.

apostle supposedly laid the 'foundations of universalism' in his letter to the Galatians: 'There is neither Jew nor Greek, neither slave nor free, neither male nor female.'[21] Slavoj Žižek, for his part, elaborates the parallels between Paul and Lenin into three pairs of guides: Christ/Paul, Marx/Lenin and Freud/Lacan. But his main point in *On Belief* (2001) is to argue the authentic ethical value of unconditional belief – political rather than religious – making no compromises and including what Kierkegaard called 'the religious suspension of ethics'. The ruthlessness of Lenin and of radical religious fundamentalists is thus presented as admirable. The Book of Job has also become a topic of fascination for Žižek, as 'perhaps the first modern critique of ideology'.[22] Meanwhile, in *Empire*, Michael Hardt and Antonio Negri hold out as an illumination of 'the future life of communist militancy' the milder religious example of Saint Francis of Assisi.[23] In his own sober way, Jürgen Habermas has also paid his respects to religion: 'As long as no better words for what religion can say are found in the medium of rational discourse, it [communicative reason] will . . . coexist abstemiously with the former, neither supporting it nor combating it.'[24] Habermas has gone even further, accepting claims that his conception of language and communicative action 'nourishes itself from the legacy of Christianity'.[25] 'For me', he writes, 'the basic concepts of philosophical ethics . . . fail to capture all the intuitions that have already found a more nuanced expression in the language of the Bible.'[26]

When the Soviet Union was crumbling, the German

---

21. Galatians 3: 28, quoted in A. Badiou, *Saint Paul: The Foundation of Universalism*, Stanford: Stanford University Press, 2003, 9.
22. S. Žižek and G. Daly, *Conversations with Žižek*, Cambridge: Polity, 2004, 161.
23. M. Hardt and A. Negri, *Empire*, Cambridge, MA: Harvard University Press, 2000, 413.
24. J. Habermas, *Religion and Rationality*, Cambridge, MA: MIT Press, 2002, 24.
25. Ibid., 160.
26. Ibid., 162.

Marxist philosopher Wolfgang Fritz Haug, a dedicated admirer of Gorbachev's attempts at reform, sat down to read Augustine's *City of God* in its original Greek – that is to say, a great theologian's reflections on the fall of Rome.[27] The same work is also referred to by Hardt and Negri, who with typical stylistic acrobatics cast the church father together with the early twentieth-century American Wobblies ('From this perspective the IWW is the great Augustinian project of modern times').[28] This widespread fascination with religion and religious examples, mainly Christian, may be taken as an indicator of a broad cultural mood, for which postmodernity seems to serve as a good label. As an alternative future disappears or dims, what become important are roots, experience and background. A classical European education, a maturation in a non-secular milieu, and a middle age at a safe distance from any demands of faith make Christianity a natural historical experience to look at.

Most recently, Terry Eagleton, a tough and unrepentant Marxist literary and cultural theorist, has returned to the left-wing Catholicism of his youth, defending Christianity against atheistic onslaught and, in resonance with Latin American liberation theology, writing on Jesus Christ and the Gospels in the light of the question of social revolution.[29]

This remarkable theological genre among a section of the European intellectual Left has also recently been bolstered by Roland Boer's wide-ranging treatment of 'biblical Marxists' and Marxist grapplings with religion, from Gramsci and Bloch to Eagleton and Žižek.[30]

---

27. W. F. Haug, personal communication.
28. M. Hardt and A. Negri, *Empire*, 207.
29. See his 'Lunging, Flailing, Mispunching', *London Review of Books*, 19 October 2006, and his introduction to The Gospels in Verso's Revolutions! Series.
30. R. Boer, *Criticism of Heaven: On Marxism and Theology*, Leiden: BRILL, 2007.

American Futurism

In the much more religious US, no comparable Left theological turn is visible. There the Bible has been more or less monopolized by the Right, although the African-American Left still has powerful political preachers such as Jesse Jackson and theologian-intellectuals such as Cornel West, self-characterized as a 'Chekhovian Christian'.[31] While European leftists are referring to Christian icons of the past, their American comrades are peering ever further into the future – short-term prospects never having looked very rosy for the North American Left. Yet among some of its best minds, expectations for the future have survived both the postmodernist onslaught and the collapse of Communism, and have asserted themselves in a new futurism. It has two remarkable currents, the most striking of which is a new utopianism, and the second is systemic and apocalyptic.

In the last decade, a variety of American radical thinkers have turned their critical intelligence and creative energies towards utopia. While waiting for new forms of political agency to emerge, 'there is no alternative to Utopia', as Fredric Jameson has put it in a masterly contribution to the field, analyzing utopian fantasy and utopian writing with his characteristic critical brilliance, erudition and galactic range of associations.[32] Utopia serves a vital political function today, Jameson emphasizes, 'in that it forces us precisely to concentrate on the [utopian] break itself: a meditation on the impossible, on the unrealizable in its own right'.[33]

Jameson is only the most recent exponent in a spectacular arc of creative American utopianism, of which he stands at one pole, focusing on the utopian 'desire', its

---

31. G. Yancy, ed., *Cornel West: A Critical Reader*, Oxford: Blackwell, 2001, 347.
32. F. Jameson, *Archaeologies of the Future*, London: Verso 2006, xii.
33. Ibid., 232.

'disruption' of the future and its literary forms, above all science fiction. In quite another register, the sociologist Erik Olin Wright launched the Real Utopias Project in the early 1990s, a large-scale collective enterprise of radical drawing-board social engineering and formalized normative economics – a subgenre different from Jameson's but not as much as their contrasting styles and references may suggest. Both are fascinated by utopian imagination, one as an analyst of science *fiction*, the other as a writer and promoter of (social) *science* fiction. So far, the Real Utopias Project has produced five books, while Wright himself is writing an ambitious strategic conclusion that proposes an understanding of socialism 'as an alternative to capitalism, as a process of social empowerment over state and economy', which will be published as *Envisioning Real Utopias*.[34]

Despite its impressive scale, and defiant stand against the headwind of the times, the design of the project may look somewhat odd, particularly to northwestern Europeans. The economic sections are classically utopian in their abstract evocations of a good society and general abstention from strategic thinking about how existing society can be changed. But they are, on the other hand, often remarkably modest, perhaps overmodest, in their targets. Thus John Roemer, for instance, presents an ingenious scheme for coupon socialism, a market society where property rights are invested in the coupon-holding adult citizenry. At the same time, he finds the already existing

---

34. J. Cohen and J. Rogers, eds, *Associations and Democracy*, London: Verso, 1995; J. Roemer, ed., *Equal Shares: Making Market Socialism Work*, London: Verso, 1996; S. Bowles and H. Gintis, eds, *Recasting Egalitarianism: New Rules of Accountability and Equity in Markets, States and Communities*, London: Verso, 1998; A. Fung and E. O. Wright, eds, *Deepening Democracy: Institutional Innovations in Empowered Participatory Governance*, London: Verso, 2003; B. Ackerman, A. Alstott and P. Van Parijs, eds, *Redesigning Distribution*, London: Verso, 2006; E. O. Wright, 'Compass Points', *New Left Review* 41, Sept–Oct 2006.

Nordic redistribution by taxation too radical to emulate: 'I doubt that large heterogeneous societies will, in our lifetime, vote to redistribute income as much through the taxation system as the Nordic societies have.'[35] In another volume, devoted to basic income schemes and to 'stakeholder grants' for all young adults, a critical voice (also American) concludes the following from a comparison with actually existing Sweden: 'The fully developed welfare state deserves priority over Basic Income because it accomplishes what Basic Income does not: it guarantees that certain specific human needs will be met.'[36] As utopianism, the political aspect of the project is more innovative in that it presents and discusses, theoretically and in different voices, four actually existing experiments with local participatory democracy, ranging from Chicago to West Bengal.[37]

The geographer and urban historian David Harvey has attempted a bold 'dialectical utopianism' in *Spaces of Hope* (2000). Its proposed transcendence of the nineteenth-century gap between Marxian historical dialectics and utopian constructions may not convince everybody who is in principle sympathetic. While US-centred globalization may be in 'disarray', discrepancies between ideological promises and economic delivery, or 'difficulties' created by market externalities, hardly constitute contradictions in the Marxian sense of structural interdependencies-cum-incompatibilities.[38] However, theoretical 'correctness' is a minor point here. Harvey, who still proudly teaches Marx's *Capital*, presents some interesting utopian principles for an 'insurgent architect at work',

---

35. J. Roemer, 'A Future for Socialism', in *Equal Shares*, ed. J. Roemer, 37.
36. B. Bergmann, 'A Swedish-Style Welfare State or Basic Income? Which Should Have Priority?', in Ackerman et al., eds, *Redesigning Distribution*, 141.
37. See Fung and Wright, eds, *Deepening Democracy*.
38. D. Harvey, *Spaces of Hope*, Edinburgh: Edinburgh University Press, 2000, 193–4.

and appends a Bellamy-inspired utopian walk through Baltimore in 2020, on which he self-critically reflects.[39] Once, in its darkest hours, Central European Marxism produced a singular masterpiece on utopian thinking and 'anticipatory consciousness', Ernst Bloch's three-volume *Principle of Hope*, published in Germany in 1954 but written much earlier. In the current context, however, the genre has not been flourishing on the eastern side of the Atlantic.

In the 1990s, when most people discussing 'transitions' were thinking about the Eastern European shift from socialism to capitalism, the message came from Binghamton, New York, that the world was in fact passing from capitalism to something else, the character of which was still uncertain. 'We are living in the transition from our existing world-system, the capitalist world economy, to another world-system or systems', Immanuel Wallerstein proclaimed in *Utopistics*, a work which defined its aim as 'the sober, rational and realistic evaluation of human social systems, the constraints on what they can be, and the zones open to human creativity'.[40]

Giovanni Arrighi, then also at Binghamton, ran a parallel research project that reached similar if yet more dramatic conclusions. From his reading of world-system history, Arrighi saw three possible outcomes to the 'ongoing crisis of the regime of accumulation'[41] – firstly, that the 'old centres' terminate capitalist history 'through the formation of a truly

39. From the rich North American fascination with utopias, one should also take note of the 2000 issue of the annual *Socialist Register* on 'Necessary and Unnecessary Utopias' and the captivating twentieth-century history of East–West utopias and their passing, in S. Buck-Morss's *Dreamworld and Catastrophe*, Cambridge, MA: MIT Press, London 2000.

40. I. Wallerstein, *Utopistics*, New York: The New Press, 1998, 35, 1–2. A collective research project had already summarized the character of the times in the same terms: see *The Age of Transition: Trajectory of the World-System 1945–2025*, T. Hopkins and I. Wallerstein, eds, Atlantic Heights, NJ: Zed Books, 1996.

41. G. Arrighi, *The Long Twentieth Century*, London: Verso, 1994, 355–6.

global world empire'; secondly, that a new guard arises
but lacks the necessary 'state- and war-making
capabilities', whereupon 'capitalism (the "anti-market")
would wither away'; and thirdly, that 'capitalist history
come to an end' by being burnt up 'in the horrors (or
glory) of escalating violence'. A crucial element of the
world-system, in this view, is the role of its economic-
cum-political hegemon. The current incumbent, the US,
has been in irreversible decline since the 1970s. As in the
past, the current financial expansion of capitalism is an
expression of, and vehicle for, a profound crisis of existing
world-system hegemony. Capitalism is threatened from
two sides: by a long-term strengthening of the power of
workers – through global deruralization and proletarian-
ization – and by the weakening of states and of their
capacity for capital protection and social mediation, a
result of the discrediting and delegitimation of state
reformism (what Wallerstein calls 'liberalism').

According to Wallerstein, the principal mechanism by
which capitalists have been able to limit the 'political
pressure' caused by the secular historical trend towards
increasing working-class strength, through democratization and other channels, has been 'the relocation of given
sectors to other zones of the world economy that are on
the average lower-wage areas'. But 'the problem today is
that, after five hundred years, there are few places left to
run to'.[42] Wallerstein is here giving a new twist to Rosa
Luxemburg's 1913 argument about the breakdown of
capitalism: 'Capitalism needs non-capitalist social
organizations as the setting for its development, [but] it
proceeds by assimilating the very conditions which alone
can ensure its existence.'[43] At the time, Luxemburg was

---

42. I. Wallerstein, *The Decline of American Power: the US in a Chaotic World*,
London: W. W. Norton, 2003, 59, 228.
43. R. Luxemburg, *The Accumulation of Capital*, London: Routledge and Kegan
Paul, 1963, 446.

thinking about non-capitalist areas as necessary export markets and as providers of cheap foodstuffs.

None of those theses has attracted any wide agreement, even on the Left, in spite of the general intellectual respect for their authors. The most tangible argument, but hardly the most convincing, is the proposition that a scaling down of US power after its peaking meant a systemic crisis of world capitalism. Later formulations by Arrighi have been much less apocalyptic, and a post-American hegemony has become more plausible with the continuing rise of China and the emergence of India as a major player. The overpowering historical importance of a relay race of capitalist hegemons continues to be assumed – from Fernand Braudel – rather than unassailably argued to an audience of the not (yet) convinced. The comparative work on hegemonic transitions by Giovanni Arrighi and Beverly Silver, *Chaos and Governance in the Modern World System* (1999), concludes with a set of plausible propositions about the likely implications of a new shift, while not predicting any necessary termination of capitalism.[44] Wallerstein sticks to his long-term-transition perspective, but his analytical light seems to have become concentrated on the global geopolitics of the next twenty years rather than on systemic extinction.[45] In a comparable vein, the Egyptian economist Samir Amin's recent *Beyond US Hegemony* (2006) is a sober global analysis with a pragmatic left-wing geostrategic programme. The final step from the capitalist world-system to geopolitics and

---

44. See G. Arrighi's discussion of R. Brenner and D. Harvey in 'Tracking Global Turbulence', *New Left Review* 20, March–April 2003; 'Hegemony Unravelling – 1', *New Left Review* 32, March–April 2005; 'Hegemony Unravelling – 2', *New Left Review* 33, May–June 2005.
45. For example see I. Wallerstein, 'Entering Global Anarchy', *New Left Review* 22, July–August 2003, and 'The Curve of American Power', *New Left Review* 40, July–August 2006.

geo-economics has been taken only by the late Andre Gunder Frank, throughout his life a scholarly heretic and iconoclast: 'best forget about it [capitalism] and get on with our inquiry into the reality of universal history'.[46]

Displacements of Class

Class, formerly among the most important concepts in Left discourse, has been displaced in recent years – in part, ironically, through the latter's own defeat in the capitalist class struggle, but also because the developments of post-industrial demography have dislodged it from its previous theoretical or geographical centrality. Class persists, but without a secure abode, and with its philosophical right to existence contested. Problematizing class identity as class action deriving directly from experience, as Edward Thompson held in his marvellous and for two decades immensely influential *The Making of the English Working Class* (1963), and pointing to the importance of competing interpretations and discursive politics, as Gareth Stedman Jones and Joan Scott did in the 1980s, was originally a a way to sharpen the focus of class analysis. But twenty years later, two prominent historians who participated in the 'cultural turn' of social history have found it necessary to plead with their colleagues for an acknowledgement of 'the persistence of class as a prediscursive or nondiscursive formation'.[47]

Class remains a central descriptive category in several arenas: mainstream sociology; standard Anglo-Saxon inequality discourse, as part of the indispensable triad of class, gender and race; studies of social mobility; recent Bourdieu-inspired studies of cultural practices and

---

46. A. G. Frank, *ReOrient*, Berkeley: University of California Press, 1998, 352.
47. G. Eley and K. Nield, *The Future of Class in History*, Ann Arbor, MI: University of Michigan Press, 2007, 194.

consumption (Mike Savage et al.). But most of the links between this descriptive mainstream, on the one hand, and collective social action and radical theorizing of such action, on the other, have been snapped.

The social appearance of class has become almost unrecognizable after being dropped into the acid of pure politics, as in the political philosophy of discursive hegemony developed in Ernesto Laclau and Chantal Mouffe's *Hegemony and Socialist Strategy* (1985), arguably the most intellectually powerful contribution of post-Marxist political theory. Thus, for example, Laclau dismisses Slavoj Žižek's invocation of class and the class struggle as 'just a succession of dogmatic assertions'.[48] 'Antagonism' becomes the new central concept.

Laclau's political philosophy has been further developed in his recent *On Populist Reason* (2005), which brings together his old interest in Peronism and Latin American populism, his post-Marxist political philosophy and a newer immersion in Lacan. A heavy read at times, as a philosophy it fails to provide any tools for analyzing actual processes of social mobilization or explaining different outcomes, whether in terms of 'people' or 'class'. Its contact with the extramural world is through selected illustrations only. On the other hand, beyond the *Streit der Fakultäen* there is much in Laclau's work that rewards efforts to penetrate the sometimes dense veil of jargon. While peoples and other social forces cannot be constructed at random – limits which a philosophy of social 'logics' has difficulties coping with – it is important to bear in mind that, as Laclau points out, they are all, classes included, discursively mobilized, and that the success or failure of this mobilization is contingent; that social change brought about by resistance or insurrection

---

48. See E. Laclau, 'Structure, History, and the Political', and S. Žižek, 'Class Struggle or Postmodernism? Yes Please', in J. Butler, E. Laclau and S. Žižek, eds, *Contingency, Hegemony, Universality*, London: Verso 2000.

has an irreducible political moment of articulation and leadership; and that popular mobilizations of the excluded, the exploited or the underprivileged can take different forms, including fascist ones.

Étienne Balibar, once Althusser's star pupil, has stayed closer to the Marxist tradition. His important 1987 essay 'From the Class Struggle to the Struggle without Classes?', republished in 1997, did not answer its own question in any clearly post-Marxist mode. While stressing the wider 'universality of antagonism', Balibar also concluded that the 'class struggle can and should be thought as *one* determining structure, covering social practices, without being the *only* one.'[49]

To the recent philosophy of struggle without classes corresponds the sociology of classes without struggle. Class is well established, largely thanks to the analytical edge and empirical tenacity of John Goldthorpe, as a central concept of intergenerational mobility studies, which have become a technically advanced but intellectually isolated subdiscipline. As a category of distribution, class retains its place in sociology. Standard American sociological discourse on distribution and inequality always refers to 'class, gender and race', both in alphabetical and in non-alphabetical order. A major journal on public health, based at Johns Hopkins, pays persistent, systematic attention to class dimensions of (ill) health and mortality – though the fact that its editor, Vicente Navarro, was part of the anti-Franco underground in Spain may not be irrelevant here.

There is as yet no global class analysis corresponding to the many national class maps produced by Marxists of the 1960s and 1970s, and these earlier pictures may well be seriously challenged.[50] The reconnection of class with race

---

49. É. Balibar, *La crainte des masses*, Paris: Galilée, 1997, 242, emphasis in the original.

50. Although see, for example, K. van der Pijl on North Atlantic class relations, *Transnational Classes and International Relations*, London: Routledge, 1998; L. Sklair, *The Transnational Capitalist Class*, Oxford: WileyBlackwell, 2001; and B. Silver on the working class, *Forces of Labor*, Cambridge: Cambridge University Press, 2003.

and nation, largely suspended after the generation of Lenin and Otto Bauer, is a theoretical advance, but the emphasis is now very different.[51] Compared with 'contemporary racism', class and class emancipation are no longer central concerns. In a characteristically incisive conceptual analysis, Balibar has demonstrated the curiously under-developed position of the proletariat in *Capital*, but he has not taken it up as a challenge; his contemporary social analysis has focused rather on the issues of nation, border, citizenship and Europe.[52] On the other hand, the post-modernist onslaught has largely put an end to feminist articulations of sex and gender presented in relation to class; typically, a recent overview of 'third-wave feminism' makes no reference to class whatsoever.[53]

Europe provided the origins of the concept and the theory of class, which emerged early on the European road to modernity in internal conflicts between, on one hand, the prince the aristocracy and the higher clergy, and on the other, the Third Estate, the 'nation', the commoners, the bourgeoisie, the people. Because of its enduring Eurocentrism, Marxist theory has never properly acknowledged or taken into proper comparative account the fact that Marx and later socialists inherited a class discourse from the French Revolution and from the political economy of the British Industrial Revolution. European class mobilization and politics and European working-class movements became models for the rest of the world. Europe still has significant parties claiming to represent labour, and trade unions remain a substantial social force there. Nevertheless, in terms of analysis and social theory, class has been faring better in North America.

---

51. É. Balibar and I. Wallerstein, *Race, nation, classe*, Paris: La Découverte, 1988.
52. É. Balibar, *La crainte des masses*, 221–50; *Politics and the Other Scene*, London: Verso, 2002; *We, the People of Europe?*, Princeton, NJ: Princeton University Press, 2004.
53. S. Gillies, G. Howie and R. Munford, eds, *Third Wave Feminism*, Basingstoke: Palgrave Macmillan 2004.

The work of Erik Olin Wright has played a central role in securing a legitimate location for Marxist class analysis within academic sociology. In a characteristically elegant approach, a recent contribution structures the issue by asking, If class is the answer, what is the question? Wright discerns six types of question which will frequently have 'class' as part of their answers:

- *Distributional location*: How are people objectively located in distributions of material inequality?
- *Subjectively salient groups*: What explains how people, individually and collectively, subjectively locate themselves and others within a structure of inequality?
- *Life chances*: What explains inequalities in life chances and material standards of living?
- *Antagonistic conflicts*: What social cleavages systematically shape overt conflicts?
- *Historical variation*: How should we characterize and explain the variations across history in the social organization of inequalities?
- *Emancipation*: What sorts of transformations are needed to eliminate oppression and exploitation within capitalist societies?[54]

Wright then defines his own work, and that of Marxism generally, as primarily concerned with answering the last question, while other approaches concern themselves with the rest. The question is, however, formulated in a remarkably oblique way. It is not, for instance, What social process is crucial to the elimination of capitalist oppression and exploitation? To which the classical Marxist answer has been: class struggle. Nor is it, What are the principal forces maintaining, or capable of changing and ending, capitalist

---

54. E. O. Wright, ed., *Approaches to Class Analysis*, Cambridge: Cambridge University Press, 2005.

oppression and exploitation? To which Marxists have answered: the bourgeoisie (or the capitalist class) and the working class, respectively.

What exists of recent work on class struggles in the world tends to come from North America. Salient examples would be Beverly Silver's theoretically innovative *Forces of Labour*, or the global working-class overview in *Socialist Register 2002*. A decisive question for the future of capital and labour in the world is how strong and capable the new masses of urban labour in China, India and other large Asian countries will become.

However, there has also been a displacement, or at least a marginalization, of class in some late offshoots of world-system analysis, obscuring it with perspectives focused on continents and continental populations. Such was the implication of Gunder Frank's characteristically heretical slogan referred to above, 'Forget about capitalism'. Giovanni Arrighi is less provocative, but his major new work, pre- rather than post-Marxist, *Adam Smith in Beijing*, is ultimately concerned with relations 'among peoples of European and non-European descent', relations that Smith hoped would become more equal and mutually respectful with world trade. There is no discussion about whether new 'inter-civilizational relations' would mainly be a rapprochement of capitalists, managers and professionals across continents and civilizations, or about the prospects of a new post-Marxist slogan, 'Upper and upper-middle classes of the world, unite! You can best preserve your privileges by sticking together!'

Exits from the State

In the 1960s and 1970s, the state was a major object of contending Marxist theorization. Its current, more starkly capitalist character may have removed it from the frontier of intellectual curiosity, and most of that interest has melted away, although Claus Offe's post-Marxist critical analyses present a significant exception.[55] But there have been many different exits from the state.

Firstly, we could distinguish the move from analysis of the national capitalist state and its modes of class rule to the global network. Under the assumption that the nation-state, or at least its 'sovereignty', has declined in significance, political interest has turned to globalization and 'imperial' global networks. Insofar as this involves a step away from 'methodological nationalism',[56] the shift is warranted. However, the bold claims of loss of state sovereignty have so far never been properly empirically argued. In any time perspective longer than a few decades, it may even be seriously questioned. What was national sovereignty a hundred years ago in Africa, in Asia, in Latin America? How sovereign were the then-new Balkan states? Were not the state boundaries of travel and migration much more porous a century ago than today? Nor can the current world situation be properly understood before the position and capacity of the nation-state of the US have been seriously investigated. Perhaps a global analysis of contemporary states would be more fruitful than focusing on a stateless globe? This is not the place to answer such questions – only to take notice of their not being properly answered, or even raised, by the mainstream shift in the centre of theoretical gravity.

Another move away from the state has involved a turn to civil society, as a basis for opposition to authoritarian rule and, in more utopian visions, as the best site for new social constructions.[57] The old concept – whose distinction from the state goes back to Hegel – was revived by anti-Communist dissidence in the final years of the decomposition of Eastern European Communism. It soon gained a worldwide reception, Left and Right, as a referent for

55. C. Offe, *Modernity and the State*, Cambridge: Polity, 1996.
56. U. Beck, *Macht und Gegenmacht im globalen Zeitalter*, Frankfurt: Suhrkamp Verlag KG, 2002, ch. 2.
57. J. Keane, *Democracy and Civil Society*, London: Verso, 1988.

many different movements and strivings for civic autonomy. In Eastern Europe, civil-society discourse also had the function of keeping out any serious discussion about political economy and the restoration of capitalism – until the latter had become a *fait accompli*. Civil society as a concept has had a programmatically idealistic career, rather than having furthered analyses of variable patterns of sociability, association and collective conflict.

A third exit from state theory was provided by moving to the more abstract level of political philosophy. The autonomy or specificity of the political, in relation to modes of production and to class structures, has been a central theme of several major thinkers. A seminal work here, once again, was Laclau and Mouffe's *Hegemony and Socialist Strategy*, with its sophisticated treatment of the classical political-philosophy problem of universalism and particularism, and their discursive substitution of the hegemonic struggles of particular interests for the struggle of classes. Drawn from completely different sources of philosophical inspiration, Habermas's grand theory of communicative action presented a normative programme of a universalistic dialogical politics.[58]

Former disciples of Louis Althusser have made distinctive new contributions to radical political philosophy.[59] Balibar, the most circumspect and perhaps the most influential among them, has brought skilled textual readings to bear both on pre-Marxian political philosophy (Spinoza, Rousseau, Locke, Fichte) and on the political theorization

58. J. Habermas, *The Theory of Communicative Action*, 2 vols, Boston, MA: Beacon Press, 1984–87. In an interesting abstention from argument, Laclau and Mouffe dismiss Habermas's ideal of a non-exclusive public sphere of rational argument as a 'conceptual impossibility'. A tyranny of concepts? See E. Laclau and C. Mouffe, *Hegemony and Socialist Strategy*, 2nd edition, London: Verso, 2000, xvii.

59. J. Rancière, *Aux bords du politique*, Paris: Gallimard 1990; É. Balibar, *Masses, Classes, Ideas*, New York: Routledge 1994; A. Badiou, 'Politics and Philosophy: An Interview with Alain Badiou', appendix to A. Badiou, *Ethics*, London: Verso, 2001.

of violent antagonisms. Alongside the traditional left-wing politics of emancipation and transformation, Balibar has reflected on a politics of 'civility', regulating 'the conflict of identifications'.[60] Violence here appears more physically tangible and more ambiguous, even dubious, in meaning, rather than in the cathartic form discussed by Sartre and Fanon.

While the anticapitalist nature of his project is very explicit and his philosophical erudition conspicuous, Slavoj Žižek's political philosophy appears more like a stance than a reasoned deduction. A compulsively productive writer and formidable polemicist, with a seemingly inexhaustible supply of cinematic and other contemporary cultural aperçus, Žižek has become an emblematic figure of contemporary radical iconoclasm. His Tito-era Slovenian background, as a former Communist turned anti-Communist dissident, provides him at the same time with a classical left-wing political formation and with impeccably respectable liberal credentials. This combination has in recent years made Žižek the only Leninist with an admiring Western following.[61] Like that of most other radical philosophers today, Žižek's anticapitalist project is very vague; this provoked an ill-tempered exchange between him and Laclau, each accusing the other of a political project meaning 'nothing at all'.[62] More noteworthy is an acknowledged ambivalence in Žižek's political position. His fascination with Lenin is accompanied by a seemingly equivalent admiration of the 'authentic conservative' who, like the British Empire Tories admired by Kipling, is not afraid of the 'necessary dirty work'.[63]

---

60. É. Balibar, *La crainte des masses*, ch. 1.

61. S. Žižek, ed., *Revolution at the Gates*, London: Verso, 2002.

62. E. Laclau, 'Structure, History and the Political', in Butler et al., eds, *Contingency, Hegemony, Universality*, 206; S. Žižek, 'Holding the Place', ibid., 321.

63. S. Žižek, *The Ticklish Subject*, London: Verso, 1999, 236; *Conversations with Žižek*, 50–1.

Marxist state theory was more than anything else a critique of capitalist democracy, and had its sharpest analytical edge when capitalism was trying to take cover under liberal democracy. Since about 1980, it has felt no need of such drapery, asserting itself in its own right and explicitly seeking to rein in existing liberal democracy by making central banks independent of it and by trying to restrict economic policy options a priori by constitutional or equivalent clauses. Under the impact of this, as well as the impact of globalization discourse on the new impotence of the state, radical political thought has paid increasing attention to potentials for 'radical democracy', a project pushed by the philosopher Chantal Mouffe and best manifested by the lusophone legal-cum-political theory developed by the Brazilian Roberto Mangabeira Unger and the Portuguese Boaventura de Sousa Santos.

It should be added that while (post-)Marxists have played truant from the state, sterling contributions to analyzing the making of the European nation-states have been made from different perspectives by Michael Mann and Charles Tilly.[64]

Return of Sexuality

The distinction between (biological) sex and (social) gender was first elaborated by Ann Oakley in 1972, and the question of the construction and transformation of gender constituted a key theoretical focus for socialist and mainstream feminism in the 1970s and 1980s.[65] But the givenness of sex has more recently come under attack, sometimes in ways similar to the questioning of any non-discursive givenness of class. The intellectual reassertion

---

64. M. Mann, *The Sources of Social Power*, vol. 2, Cambridge: Cambridge University Press, 1993; C. Tilly, *Coercion, Capital and European States, AD 990–1990*, Oxford: WileyBlackwell, 1990.
65. A. Oakley, *Sex, Gender and Society*, London: MT Smith, 1972.

of sexuality has come from the American philosopher Judith Butler – 'sex itself is a gendered category'[66] – and in theorizations from the French battleground of philosophy and psychoanalysis.[67] Oakley herself has conceded the untenability of the sex–gender distinction.[68] Politically, the givenness of sex has been powerfully challenged by assertive homosexuality. The latter has achieved a certain specific theoretical presence in Anglo-Saxon academia under the banner of 'queer theory'. In a large body of theory, inequalities between heterosexual men and women have been overshadowed by discourses on homo- and transsexuality, constituting new though extremely minoritarian theoretical fields. Again, the displacement of gender has a noteworthy similarity with the displacement of class. While raising awareness of human and social complexity in important ways, neither tendency is likely, *qua* displacement, to be a helpful contribution to human emancipation.

The surge of literary-philosophical postmodernism in feminist discourse broke most of the links between feminist theory and the Left that had earlier come under the heading of socialist feminism.[69] Scandinavian welfare-state-oriented feminists experienced the encounter with postmodernist feminism as a shock.[70] The cosmopolitan literary theorist Toril Moi has felt compelled to provide an answer to the question 'What is a woman?' for academic feminist milieux

---

66. J. Butler, *Gender Trouble*, New York: Routledge, 1990, 7.
67. K. Oliver, *French Feminism Reader*, Oxford: Rowman & Littlefield, 2000; D. Cavallaro, *French Feminist Theory: An Introduction*, London 2003.
68. A. Oakley, 'A Brief History of Gender', in *Who's Afraid of Feminism?*, A. Oakley and J. Mitchell, eds, London: Continuum, 1997, 29–55.
69. See A. Oakley and J. Mitchell, eds, *Who's Afraid of Feminism?* For a global materialist account of sex, gender and reproductive relations over the past century, see G. Therborn, *Between Sex and Power: Family in the World, 1900–2000*, London: Routledge, 2004.
70. Hildur Ve and Karin Waerness, oral communication.

apparently disoriented as to the answer.[71] Yet it is also striking that feminism is today far more salient than the Left in the Euro-American world.

The return of sexuality is also manifest in current Marxist and post-Marxist philosophy, in its eager preoccupation with psychoanalysis. Žižek was trained as a Lacanian; Laclau's recent work on populism is much interested in Lacan's *objet petit a* and other topics of the master. Belatedly, Balibar has followed his teacher, Althusser, into studies of Freud and Lacan – for instance in his 'Three Concepts of Politics' – albeit in a cautious and selective manner.[72]

Homage to Networks

Classical nineteenth-century sociological theory focused on modes of social connectivity, distinguishing 'association' from 'community'. Mid-twentieth-century sociology concentrated on the 'group', whether 'primary' or 'secondary', and on organizations. More recently, the *network* has replaced the concept of structure or organization in social theory. Network analysis of social connectivity has a background in social psychology, above all in the 'sociometric' studies of friendships in school milieux and in postwar community studies by anthropologists and family sociologists. The concept was also used in US studies of the diffusion of ideas. From the 1960s on, it was used to develop mathematical models for access, diffusion and power structures in an expanding number of areas, from vacancy chains to sexual contacts and global city patterns. The key theoretical figures have been Harrison White and his students.[73] The notion of the network reached a wider public in the 1980s

---

71. T. Moi, *Sex, Gender and Body*, Oxford: Oxford University Press, 2005.

72. É. Balibar, *Masses, Classes, Ideas*, ch. 7; *Politics and the Other Scene*.

73. H. White, *Identity and Control*, Princeton, NJ: Princeton University Press, 1992; J. Rule, *Theory and Progress in Social Science*, Cambridge: Cambridge University Press, 1997, ch. 5.

through business-management studies that attempted to grasp and generalize the success of Toyota and other Japanese corporations. Further interest was stimulated, of course, by the electronic revolution and the Internet. Michael Mann made 'networks of interaction' a central, though loosely used, concept in his monumental work on power, with a view to avoiding any systemic or bounded notion of 'society'.[74]

Networks are looser and more open than both groups and organizations. They focus on individual actors and their resources, rather than on constituted collectivities, and they form channels for markets as well as for bureaucracies, movements and classes. As such, networks are highly important social connections, tying together complex, loosely coupled social systems. Their rise to centre-stage in contemporary social theory and analysis should be seen not only as deriving from intellectual discovery, but also as indicating changes in social relations. It was the post-Marxist sociologist Manuel Castells who articulated the 'network society' in a magisterial work of social analysis, setting out from new management conceptions and information technology without trying to relate it to previous sociological theory.[75] Since then it has become a key analytical concept in the influential neo-Marxist enterprise of Hardt and Negri's *Empire* (2000) and *Multitude* (2004), in which both the global sovereign and its opposition are presented as network powers. On the other hand, while crucial to recent post- and neo-Marxist social theorizing, the 'network' itself has no political affiliation. Nor has it been subjected to any analytical critique or any scrutiny of its relative acumen and the

---

74. M. Mann, *Sources of Social Power*, Cambridge: Cambridge University Press, 1986–. Two volumes have been published thus far.
75. M. Castells, *The Information Age: Economy, Society and Culture*, 3 vols, Oxford: WileyBlackwell, 1996–98.

boundaries of its indubitable fruitfulness. It is a concept still enjoying its honeymoon undisturbed.

Political Economies

European 'Western Marxism' had always regarded political economy from something of a distance, and it is not surprising that this should have widened over recent decades. Exceptions to the rule endure, among them the ecologically oriented world-economic analyses of Elmar Altvater.[76] Until his premature death a few years ago, Egon Matzner carried on the classical Central European Marxist tradition of economic analysis. Anglo-Saxon radicalism, by contrast, has always contained a strong current of critical political economy, Marxist as well as non-Marxist. While the spirited and forceful engagement with liberal economics by British left-wing neo-Ricardians of the 1960s – the aforementioned Cambridge, England, versus Cambridge, Massachusetts, debate on capital theory – does not seem to have sustained any enduring encroachments on the dominion and self-confidence of liberalism, radical political economy in the Anglo-Saxon world is still very productive. Its major achievements in recent years have tended to derive from creative disciplinary cross-fertilizations of economics and history, economics and political science, and economics and philosophy.

Self-consciously heterodox, world-systems analysis has been a vital force for critical social analysis. Developed from the mid-1970s by Wallerstein and others, and currently being extended in new directions by Arrighi, it has also proved stimulating to colleagues outside, and often in disagreement with, the school. Though pioneered by sociologists, the analysis is predominantly economic

---

76. For example, E. Altvater, *Der Preis des Wohlstands oder Umweltplünderung und neue Welt(un)ordnung*, Münster: Verlag Westfalisches Dampfboot, 1992.

and historical, while its attention to global power relations adds a crucial political dimension. To date, it has proved a more fruitful approach than recent plunges into theories of globalization. With a unique sense of the limits of the self in history, Wallerstein has already warned his followers and collaborators of the project's coming demise; the basis for his prediction was precisely its degree of success and its implicit recognition as a viable global analysis.[77] One may add that once the planetary world has been recognized as a central, indeed as the most important, focus for social analysis, the rise of a number of different approaches to global studies is to be expected.

The imminent-end-of-capitalism theses of Arrighi and Wallerstein have been noted above. Two other major, much more down-to-earth combinations of economics and history avoid epochal power-shift theses or speculations. Robert Brenner, who first made his name with an account of the origins of capitalism so striking and iconoclastic as to engender 'the Brenner debate', discussed in chapter 2, has now produced an economic history of postwar advanced capitalism, *The Economics of Global Turbulence* (2006).[78] The driving analytical forces here – powering through a wealth of empirical detail and its temporal vicissitudes – are the tendency to overcapacity and a decline in profit rate. From Oxford, the late Andrew Glyn has provided a succinct and highly readable overview of recent capitalist development and its effects on human welfare.[79] Brenner envisages continuing turbulence; Glyn saw declining prospects for rich-country workers and ended by questioning the

77. I. Wallerstein, 'The Rise and Future Demise of World-Systems Analysis', *Review*, xxi: 1, 1998.
78. See T. H. Aston and C. H. E. Philpin, eds, *The Brenner Debate*, Cambridge: Cambridge University Press, 1985; R. Brenner, *The Economics of Global Turbulence*, London: Verso, 2006.
79. A. Glyn, *Capitalism Unleashed*, Oxford: Oxford University Press, 2006.

meaning of further growth, opting for that curious utopia of resignation, the 'Basic Income'.

Arrighi has recently returned to Adam Smith in his major work on the new significance of China, the aforementioned *Adam Smith in Beijing*. In a convincing rereading of *The Wealth of Nations*, Arrighi shows how Smith the market economist was enveloped by Smith the Enlightenment moral philosopher concerned with global justice. Secondly, Arrighi argues that the failure of the Project for a New American Century and the rise of China have brought the world closer to inter-national, inter-civilizational equality 'than it ever was'. This is not just because of the size and velocity of Chinese economic growth, but also because of its character, driven by market opportunities without dispossession of the direct producers on the land and by intensive, low-cost but healthy and educated labour.

The Chinese economy took off from the late 1970s with household agrarian production and with Township and Village Enterprises for the (domestic) market, without dispossessing the rural population of their means of subsistence, which is a different path of development from that of European capitalism. But whether this warrants Arrighi's historical and contemporary extrapolations is more doubtful. Starting from an analysis of recent China, Arrighi argues that '[t]he separation of agricultural producers from the means of production has been more a consequence of capitalism's creative destruction than one of its preconditions',[80] as Robert Brenner also has argued. Current Chinese manufacturing triumphs certainly appear to be based on the labour of a dispossessed working class, occasionally even falling into slavelike conditions, while rural education and health care are, at least to some extent, falling by the

---

80. G. Arrighi, *Adam Smith in Beijing*, New York: Verso, 2007, 365

wayside with the introduction of fees which put them beyond the reach of the poor. Arrighi has written a tour de force, but in the twenty-first century, national models of progressive political economy have become much harder to sell.

A recent, highly ambitious project at Santa Fe aims to produce a radical political economy by bringing together economics and political science. So far, its main output is *Globalization and Egalitarian Redistribution*, edited by Pranab Bardhan (an economist at Berkeley), Samuel Bowles (an economist and the director of the Behavioral Sciences Program at the Santa Fe Institute) and Michael Wallerstein (a political scientist at Yale). For all its equations and diagrams, the work's 'lessons' on the possibilities for redistributive policies under global constraints – fairly substantial, the editors conclude – may not be that novel. But it is also noteworthy for two other reasons: first, the power of its political-cum-economic modelling, on which one participant, Adam Przeworski, has proved masterful, previously within an explicitly Marxist approach; and second, the generous mainstream economic backing – from the Russell Sage Foundation – for a project on 'Persistent Inequality in a Competitive World'.

The main straddler of economics and philosophy is probably Amartya Sen, but there have been many interfaces between analytical philosophy and analytical economics. The turn of John Roemer from mathematical economics to 'radical economic ethics' – from *A General Theory of Exploitation and Class* (1982) to *Theories of Distributive Justice* (1996) – is an interesting trajectory and remains, from a Left viewpoint, an honourable one. Economics and sociology were brought together in *Les structures sociales de l'économie*, one of the last major works of Pierre Bourdieu. A penetrating investigation of the French housing market, it deploys some of his key concepts, such as the 'habitus' of dispositions and the 'field' of force and conflict, both in the empirical research and in a generalizing theoretical critique.[81] In *Banking on Death* and *Age Shock*, Robin Blackburn has produced an ambitious left-of-centre recasting of pension strategy for an ageing society, which builds on Rudolf Meidner's proposal for a share levy from corporations to finance social development.[82]

Political economy also includes what is usually labelled 'institutional economics', non-Marxist but usually left-of-centre. Many of its modern classics are now submerged under neoliberal lava: Ragnar Frisch, Gunnar Myrdal, Jan Tinbergen. But below the pantheon there is still a vibrant subculture of critical institutional economics. In its main centres, Britain and France, this is still largely situated within economics, but also benefits from elements of sociological inquiry. In France, the main school has been 'regulation theory'; central representatives have included Michel Aglietta, Robert Boyer and Antoine Rebérioux.[83] In Britain, the post-Marxist Geoffrey Hodgson has returned to consider the relations between economics and history, as well as evolutionary theory.[84]

THE REPERTOIRE OF POSITIONS

Social theorizing is still related to – indeed, committed to – specific political positions, and a sociological history of the field must give some account of these, while steering clear of the twin temptations of apology and denunciation.

---

81. P. Bourdieu, *Les structures sociales de l'économie*, Paris: Seuil, 2000.

82. R. Blackburn, *Banking on Death*, London: Verso, 2002; *Age Shock: How Finance is Failing Us*, London: Verso, 2006.

83. M. Aglietta and A. Rebérioux, *Corporate Governance Adrift*, Cheltenham, UK: Edward Elgar Publishing, 2005; R. Boyer and Y. Saillard, eds, *Théorie de la régulation*, Paris: La Découverte, 1995; J. R. Hollingsworth and R. Boyer, eds, *Contemporary Capitalism: The Embeddedness of Institutions*, Cambridge: Cambridge University Press, 1997.

84. G. Hodgson, *After Marx and Sraffa*, Basingstoke, UK: Palgrave Macmillan, 1991; G. Hodgson, M. Itoh and N. Yokokawa, *Capitalism in Evolution*, Cheltenham, UK: Edward Elgar Publishing, 2001.

Figure 3.1: Current Left Theoretico-Political Positions

Figure 3.1 distinguishes two poles, in relation to which the politics of recent left-wing thought might be located. One is theoretical: Marx and Marxism, as an intellectual tradition. The other is political: socialism, whose goal is a social order distinctively different from capitalism. ('Socialism' has looser meanings too, but they do not pertain here.) The two axes form a system of coordinates, which may be deployed as a heuristic searching device, though the results should not be seen as a permanent address book.

The diagram should, of course, be seen as a very approximate map, aiming to convey relative positions correctly but making no claims about the scale of distances. What it shows first of all is that theory and politics are two different dimensions, even among politically committed social theorists. Secondly, it suggests a new distance from socialism, in the sense of a distinctive, actually attainable type of society. Elaborating a conception of a socialist alternative has become a minority concern among the intellectual Left, although this does not, in most cases, imply a step into the capitalist fold.

In a continental comparison, left-of-centre intellectual currents in North America, both Marxist and non-Marxist, tend to be more to the left of Figure 3.1's meridian than their European equivalents. On the whole, the resilience of the small North American Left stands out in comparison with the larger but much softer and more often disheartened forces of Europe. It is the US that has produced such intransigent left-wing best-selling writers as Noam Chomsky and, more recently, Mike Davis.[85] The annual *Socialist Register* was launched in the mid-1960s as a very British enterprise, but is now, in the new millennium, edited from Toronto. The classical left-wing journals of the US, like *Monthly Review* and *Science and Society*, may now be shadows of their former selves, but they have survived. The huge American academic culture is still capable of sustaining a range of Left publications. Recent meetings of the American Sociological Association have been much more explicitly radical than the European meetings. (True, European left-wing academics have more opportunities for extramural practice.) The great 'right turn' occurred earlier in the US, with elements of the 1940s and 1950s *trotskisant* Left becoming cold warriors by the early 1970s, spawning a generation of rabid neoconservatives. The remainder of the American Left was never hopeful about the immediate future, and would also be further removed from the blows and reverberations of the Soviet implosion, the defeats of Eurocommunism and the surrenders of Eurosocialism.

Postsocialism

If a certain distance from any explicit socialism has characterized most of the Euro-American Left recently, the elaboration of a postsocialist left-of-centre agenda has

---

85. N. Chomsky, *Deterring Democracy*, New York: Verso, 1991; M. Davis, *Planet of Slums*, London: Verso, 2006.

become a specific project. The wasteland of triumphant Thatcherism was a natural breeding-ground for 'postsocialism'. One effort was John Keane's celebration of 'civil society', as scornful of social democracy and its 'unworkable model of state-administered socialism' as it was of 'totalitarian communism'.[86] In the last years of the Cold War this position was riding high; a decade of capitalist immiseration of large parts of Eastern Europe following 1989 elicited no qualification, or even comment, from the author.[87]

A few years later, the sociological theorist Anthony Giddens proclaimed his move 'Beyond Left and Right' in a book full of Thatcherite sneers at social democracy and the welfare state.[88] Brusquely dismissing the notion that there could be any 'third way' in the classic leftist sense – between 'welfare socialism' and 'Communism' – Giddens in fact turned out to have prepared the ground for a short-lived but nevertheless contemporarily unique politico-theoretical postsocialist alliance that was soon, in its turn, dubbed the 'Third Way'. For some years, Giddens became the officious theoretician of the British prime minister and his New Labour regime, giving an intellectual gloss to a party that had lost – or rather severed – any connection to 'first way' social democracy, in the wake of a series of traumatizing defeats dealt by a ruthless (though always civically minoritarian) neoliberalism. For a time, this project did comprise a genuine relation between social theory and politics, although of a different kind to that presupposed by the Marxist-socialist 'triangle' discussed above. It should be noted that, in Europe at least (there may still be some East Asian interest), the attractions of the Third Way ended with the *Realpolitik*

---

86. J. Keane, *Democracy and Civil Society*, 26.
87. J. Keane, 'Introduction to the New Edition', *Democracy and Civil Society*.
88. A. Giddens, *Beyond Left and Right*, Cambridge: Polity, 1994, 73ff.

of invading tanks – although in contrast to Czechoslovakia in 1968, the tanks were headed out of the country and into Iraq, with the Blair government a leading force in the aggression.[89] Ideological controversy aside, Giddens's defence of the Third Way six years later provided an exemplary summary, accurate yet concise, of the most important criticisms that had been levelled against it, to which he responded with a wide range of social-scientific references.[90] A sometime collaborator of Giddens, Ulrich Beck is a radical cosmopolitan democrat, for whom the Communism and socialism of Europe's 'first modernity' are now 'used-up' ideas.[91]

The 1998 autodissolution of Italy's Democratic Party of the Left and its eventual merger into the Democratic Party in 2007 constitute, at least in form, even more of a disavowal of social-democratic leanings than the Blair–Brown project of 'New Labour'. Its courtier-theorist does not seem to be in sight yet.

Non-Marxist Left

Social democracy, by far the major component of the non-Marxist Left, has produced few theoreticians of wide ambition in recent years. The work of the Swedish sociologist Walter Korpi has largely centred on empirical analysis of social-policy institutions, but his explanatory

---

89. Postsocialism has also had a generational dimension. In 1994, Ralph Miliband died; a prominent Marxist political scientist, author of *The State in Capitalist Society* (1969), Miliband's unrepentant *Socialism for a Sceptical Age* (1994) was published posthumously. In the same year his son, David, who was to become foreign secretary, edited an anthology, *Reinventing the Left*, in which Giddens tabled a postsocialist agenda.
90. A. Giddens, *The Third Way*, Cambridge: Polity, 1998; *The Third Way and Its Critics*, Cambridge: Polity, 2000.
91. V. Beck, *Risk Society*; and *Macht und Gegenmacht*, 407.

theorizations of power resources and the 'democratic class struggle', together with his scientifically robust defence of the welfare state, are important contributions to social theory.[92] Politically, too, Korpi has remained a staunch social democrat. Scandinavian social democracy has had its share of recent defeats and demoralizations, hitting the Danes above all. But on the whole, it is still a major force left-of-centre.

French sociology has generally remained 'left-of-centre', even while the media and the principal intellectual platforms in Paris have veered sharply to the right.[93] During the 1990s, the most outstanding contribution was that of Pierre Bourdieu. Out of the spotlight in the heyday of rue d'Ulm Marxism, Bourdieu built up a formidable reputation as a top-class social researcher before emerging late in life as the foremost intellectual spokesman of the anti-capitalist Left, not only in France but in Europe generally. His was a powerful voice against the capitalist 'misery of the world' – even though he did not hold out the prospect of a socialist horizon, nor did he ever condone the existing order.[94]

There has been little radical programmatic thinking in social democracy anywhere since the ambitious but politically ill-fated wage-earner-funds proposal by the Swedish blue-collar unions, for a while reluctantly adopted by the Swedish Social Democratic Party. Most distressing has been the absence of any significant social-democratic visions in Eastern Europe. It is instead a Brazilian-American legal philosopher, Roberto Mangabeira Unger,

92. W. Korpi, *The Democratic Class Struggle*, London: Routledge, 1983; W. Korpi and J. Palme, 'The Paradox of Redistribution and Strategies of Equality', *American Sociological Review* 63: 5, 1998.
93. A. Touraine, *Beyond Neoliberalism*, Oxford: Polity, 2001.
94. P. Bourdieu et al., *La misère du monde*, Paris: La Seuil, 1993 (*The Weight of the World*, Stanford 1999); P. Bourdieu, *Contre-feux*, Paris: Liber-Raions d'agir, 1998 (*Firing Back: Against the Tyranny of the Market*, New York: New Press, 2003).

who has had the imagination to write *What Should the Left Propose?* – an answer to that very question. His appeal to the petty-bourgeois longing 'for a condition of modest prosperity and independence' and to a 'universal desire' for 'national sovereignty' may sound timid. But his proposals for institutional change are potentially far-reaching. These are guided by five 'institutional ideas': high domestic savings and taxation as a basis for national independence; social policy based on empowerment and capacity; democratization of the market economy and achievement of 'an upward tilt in the return to labour'; a universal responsibility for caring work; and a 'high-energy democratic politics'.[95]

The World Social Forums, one of the most important and inspiring developments in left-wing politics in the new millennium, have so far spawned little social theory; the Portuguese legal scholar Boaventura de Sousa Santos has, however, made a sterling contribution in trying to analyze and interpret this complex and heterogeneous movement.[96] At the same time, themes of inequality or working conditions under capitalism, long central to the Left, have also been theorized in radical ways outside it. The contrasting approaches of Richard Sennett, highly literary and descriptive, and of Charles Tilly, always rigorously systematic, provide two powerful examples.[97] Radical social theory remains a big house, with many doorways.

---

95. R. Mangabeira Unger, *What Should the Left Propose?*, London: Verso, 2005, 166, 24–31.
96. See the Verso series, *Reinventing Social Emancipation: Towards New Manifestos*, London: Verso, 2006 and forthcoming.
97. R. Sennett, *Respect in a World of Inequality*, New York: Allen Lane, 2003; R. Sennett, *The Culture of the New Capitalism*, New Haven, CT: Yale University Press, 2006; C. Tilly, *Durable Inequality*, Berkeley: University of California Press, 1998; D. McAdam, S. Tarrow and C. Tilly, *Dynamics of Contention*, Cambridge: Cambridge University Press, 2001.

Marxology and Scientific Marxism

The northeastern quadrant of Figure 3.1 is not necessarily empty. It is logically possible, today more than ever, to abstain from any anticapitalist practice or ideological stance while nonetheless finding Marx to be an insightful and intellectually stimulating analyst of capitalism. *Pace* Burawoy and Wright, such a position is not necessarily degenerate, cynical or pessimistic.[98] Given the normal cultural-political embeddedness of social science, however, we should expect this field to be very sparsely populated. The most salient contemporary example of this position is the Indian-British economist Meghnad Desai, appointed by Tony Blair to the House of Lords. With the help of its library, he has written a spirited account of the dynamics of capitalism, in which Marx joins hands with Hayek. *Marx's Revenge* (2002) is a rehabilitation of Marx the social scientist of capitalist political economy, originally inspired by a rereading of Lenin and the classical Marxist economists, while taking an agnostic position as to whether any postcapitalist social order is possible. Here we may also situate British Academy Marxist historiography.

The last years of the twentieth century saw two remarkable synthetic readings of Marx: *Specters of Marx* by Jacques Derrida (1993) and *The Postmodern Marx* by Terrell Carver (1998). Derrida and Carver both saw Marx*es*, in the plural; both underlined, in a sympathetic yet critical way, the political significance of Marx, but as a historical figure, out of joint with the Marxism of any contemporary movements. Derrida now placed his own whole *oeuvre* of deconstruction 'within a certain tradition of Marxism, within a certain spirit of Marxism', while illuminating his

---

98. M. Burawoy and E. O. Wright, 'Sociological Marxism', in *Handbook of Sociological Theory*, ed. J. Turner, New York: Springer, 2002, 484.

reading with literary pyrotechnics.[99] Carver's postmodernism was a 'mild' one, which did not confront modernity or the Enlightenment and manifested itself mainly in a perceptive analysis of Marx's language and writing strategies in various texts.[100]

Post-Marxism

Post-Marxism is used here in an open sense, referring to writers with an explicitly Marxist background, whose recent work has gone beyond Marxist problematics and who do not publicly claim a continuing Marxist commitment. It is not tantamount to ex-Marxism, nor does it include denunciation or renegacy; development and new desires, yes, maybe even divorce, but only on amicable terms. The boundaries between post- and neo-Marxism have become blurred in recent times, and some important writers – Étienne Balibar, for example – may well be listed under both rubrics. Here, no critical evaluation is invested in the grouping; however, the term 'neo-Marxist' will be used only for theoretical projects which both signal a significant departure from classical Marxism and retain an explicit commitment to it.

Laclau and Mouffe, accepting a post-Marxist label, refer to 'the reappropriation of an intellectual tradition, as well as the process of going beyond it'.[101] *Hegemony and Socialist Strategy*, discussed above, may be regarded as one of the most important contributions from this position. Deploying a series of formidable abstractions, the authors toil through classical Marxist political theory, from German and Russian social democracy to Gramsci. But the crux of their project

---

99. J. Derrida, *Spectres de Marx*, 151. See also the discussion of Derrida's book in *Ghostly Demarcations*, ed. M. Sprinker, London: Verso, 1999.
100. T. Carver, *The Postmodern Marx*, Manchester: Manchester University Press, 1998, 2.
101. E. Laclau and C. Mouffe, *Hegemony and Socialist Strategy*, ix.

remains the French Revolution – in itself a venerable tradition, from Marx and Lenin to Gramsci – and the call for 'radical democracy', in which a 'socialist dimension' is to be achieved by 'deepening the democratic revolution'.

German critical theory was arguably the first major current of post-Marxism, politically implicit in the frozen silence of Adorno and Horkheimer after the Second World War, loftily explicit in the work of Jürgen Habermas. As a post-Marxist, Habermas has remained an intellectual and theoretician of a liberal (in the American sense) Left, becoming a left-of-centre conscience of the West German nation – far less radical than Sartre but more widely hearkened to. In recent years, he has grappled with the moral issues surrounding genetic engineering and has struggled to come to terms with the increasingly violent and disagreeable implications of a *Westbindung* with the US – a bond to which Habermas, as a German anti-nationalist, has always been committed. In the context of the invasion of Iraq, there occurred an interesting, more Europeanist rapprochement between Habermas and Derrida.[102] For this overview, however, it is Habermas's programme of dialogical politics – laid out in his magnum opus on communicative action – and his defence of modernity as an 'unfinished project' that have to be underlined.[103] Claus Offe, once Habermas's student, and a long-time post-Marxist, is one of the few who, as a prominent political scientist, has continued the 1960s–70s Marxist preoccupation with the state, among other things taking it into the post-Communist states of Eastern Europe.[104]

The current professorial successor of the Frankfurt School is Axel Honneth. His most important work has

102. G. Borradori, *Philosophy in a Time of Terror: Dialogues with Jürgen Habermas and Jacques Derrida*, Chicago: University of Chicago Press, 2003.
103. J. Habermas, *Theory of Communicative Action; Der Philosophische Diskurs der Moderne*.
104. C. Offe, *Modernity and the State*.

concerned the struggle for recognition, initiated as a topic for modern social philosophy by Hegel's analysis of the dialectic of the master–slave relation. Honneth has further differentiated this into three spheres: love, law and solidarity.[105] In a debate with the American philosopher Nancy Fraser, who was spurred by strident US 'identity politics' into defending redistribution, Honneth argued for a normative theory of experiences of injustice that would be broader than the 'more or less utilitarian anthropology' of Marxism.[106] From an egalitarian perspective, as I have argued elsewhere, 'recognition' may be seen as a crucial aspect of existential equality, one of three fundamental dimensions of (in)equality; given Honneth's background, the modernist optimism of his observations on 'moral progress' may also be worth noting.[107]

Post-Marxism has not been limited to textual reinterpretation; it may equally well take the form of new empirical forays or social commentary. Two of the most extraordinary works to emerge from a Marxist background are the landmark sociological analysis of world society by Manuel Castells, noted above, and the strikingly ambitious historical 'mediology' of Régis Debray. The latter begins from a critique of the Marxist concept of ideology, and an engagement with the Althusserian discussion of 'ideological state apparatuses', opening out onto a *longue durée* exploration of the materiality of mediated communication, or the 'mechanics of [cultural] transmission', with a particular focus on Judaism and Christianity.[108]

105. A. Honneth, *The Struggle for Recognition: The Moral Grammar of Social Conflict*, Cambridge, MA: Polity, 1995.
106. N. Fraser and A. Honneth, *Redistribution or Recognition?*, London: Verso 2003, 127.
107. G. Therborn, 'Understanding and Explaining Inequality', in Therborn, ed., *Inequalities of the World*, London: Verso, 2006, 186ff.
108. R. Debray, *Media Manifestos*, London: Verso, 1996; *Transmitting Culture*, New York: Columbia University Press, 2000.

Theoretically original and skilfully crafted, these works are first of all contributions to social analysis rather than to social theory; as such, they are outstanding achievements. Finally, the prolific output of social commentary by Zygmunt Bauman has had a strong transnational resonance; at heart, this is a sociological variety of post-modernism. Bauman's recent writings travel light, burdened neither by research nor by theoretical analytics, but borne up by an unusual life wisdom, a trained observer's eye and a fluent pen.[109]

Neo-Marxism

For all its political defeats, the intellectual creativity of Marxism has not come to an end. The last decade has seen the emergence of at least two highly original, hard-hitting discourses, which explicitly derive from and build upon Marxist legacies. We have already noted the irreverent philosophical politics of Slavoj Žižek, who has not only radically renewed Marxist cultural criticism but vigorously defends an iconoclastic Marxism against 'conformist liberal scoundrels'. Žižek's *oeuvre* includes a spirited defence of classical modernity and the extensive use of popular cinema in cultural-philosophical commentaries. He has flown in the face of conventional wisdom to the extent of introducing, with commentary, a new selection of Lenin's writings from 1917.[110] Žižek's exhortation to 'repeat Lenin' posits an openness to the possibilities for radical social change in an apparently hopeless situation, following disastrous defeat – in Lenin's case, the First World War and the breakup of the Second International.

---

109. Z. Bauman, *Intimations of Postmodernity*, London: Routledge, 1992; *Liquid Modernity*.
110. See respectively: *Did Somebody Say Totalitarianism?*, London: Verso, 2002, 4; *Ticklish Subject; Revolution at the Gates*.

The second major manifestation of neo-Marxism, Hardt and Negri's *Empire* and *Multitude*, claims to have found the revolutionary exit of the twenty-first century: 'This is a revolution that no power will control – because bio-power and communism, co-operation and revolution remain together, in love, simplicity, and also innocence. This is the irrepressible lightness and joy of being communist.' Or again:

> The possibility of democracy on a global scale is emerging today for the first time . . . After this long season of violence and contradictions . . . the extraordinary accumulation of grievances and reform proposals must at some point be transformed by a strong event, a radical insurrectionary demand . . . In time, an event will thrust us like an arrow into that [already] living future.[111]

Hardt and Negri also refer to the Lenin of *State and Revolution* as an inspiration for the 'destruction of sovereignty', though here combined with the Madisonian conception of checks and balances. The two bodies of work have several features in common, in addition to their upbeat radicalism and international publishing success. Both are essentially works of political philosophy – if one accepts that Žižek's main books are *The Sublime Object of Ideology* (1989) and *The Ticklish Subject* (1999) – rather than of social theory. Negri and Žižek are professional philosophers, while Negri's former Paris student Hardt is a literary theorist with a philosophical orientation. Both sets of authors write with verve and gusto in a baroque style of *assemblage*, displaying an impressive erudition and a capacity for association which encompasses a great

---

111. Respectively: M. Hardt and A. Negri, *Empire*, 413, italics omitted; *Multitude*, Cambridge, MA: Penguin Putnam, 2004, xi, 358.

number of fields and traditions, at high speed and with little time for historical contextualization or empirical investigation. Different variants of dissident Communism, and a more similar mainstream-Communist family of origin, form the political backgrounds of Negri and Žižek: respectively, the spontaneist and violent Italian Far Left, and a meandering Slovenian Communism-cum-dissidence. They are also in line with Western Marxist practice in the sense of reading and using Marx through the lenses of other great European intellectual traditions – primarily the psychoanalysis of Lacan, but also a philosophical spectrum with Heidegger at its centre in the case of Žižek, and the philosophy of Spinoza in the case of Negri. Moreover, their dazzling style as thinkers has attracted readers far removed from their own political or philosophical stance.

One of Žižek's most recent books, *The Parallax View*, presents itself as his 'most substantial work in many years'. It revolves around a well-chosen metaphor: parallax is 'the apparent displacement of an object (the shift of its position against a background) caused by a change in observational position that provides a new line of sight'. But this ambitious volume, in the author's usual style of far-ranging associations, anecdotes, cinematography and polemical shock, also shows the diminishing returns of this sort of free-wheeling critique. While Žižek still draws some interesting aperçus out of his hat, many of his thematic discussions lack both a cutting edge and analytical depth – for example, his patient rebuttal of the Lacanian Jean-Claude Milner's Zionist ranting; his respectful scepticism towards Alain Badiou's 'exalted defence' of revolutionary terror; or his Napoleonic analogy in support of his thesis of 'the historical necessity of the Stalinist outcome' of the October Revolution.[112]

---

112. S. Žižek, *The Parallax View*, Cambridge, MA: MIT Press, 2006, 253ff, 292–3, 326ff.

While Žižek may say, 'I have nothing whatsoever to do with sociology',[113] the work of Hardt and Negri does directly pertain to social analysis – their Franco-Italian philosophical mode of writing notwithstanding. Their approach centres around two key concepts, Empire and multitude, both taken from Spinoza. Hardt and Negri interpret Spinoza's *imperium* simply as sovereignty, and in their work the concept has nothing of the material concreteness of, say, the Roman or the British empires. Rather, it is a global network to which sovereign power has migrated from the nation-states, and in this sense is 'a step forward', as these authors of a self-proclaimed postmodernity assert in a typically modernist way. The concomitant to Empire is the 'multitude', which here replaces the Marxist 'proletariat' and the 'people' of classical democratic theory. The 'mass workers' of Negri's ultraleft Italy of the 1960s–70s are now writ (globally) large as 'mass intellectuality'. The multitude is similarly comprised of all the planet's workers and 'poors', now increasingly interrelated across a 'smoothed' world space of withering civil society and declining national boundaries, by common knowledge and common relationships. Its expanding practice will bring about global democracy, 'a future that is already living'. Socialism remains absent from this prophetic vision.[114]

In their emphasis on information and networks, especially as the new locus for sovereignty, there is a diagnostic similarity between Hardt and Negri's work and the empirically grounded, end-of-millennium analysis by Castells. The most important divergence between them concerns social differentiation. In contrast to one global multitude 'in an expanding, virtuous spiral' of commonality,[115] Castells defines the 'truly fundamental social cleavages of the Information Age':

---

113. S. Žižek and G. Daly, *Conversations with Žižek*, 32.
114. Respectively: M. Hardt and A. Negri, *Empire*, 43, 336; *Multitude*, 348–50, 358.
115. M. Hardt and A. Negri, *Multitude*, 350.

First, the internal fragmentation of labour between informational producers and replaceable generic labour. Secondly, the social exclusion of a significant segment of society made up of the discarded individuals whose value as workers/consumers is used up, and whose relevance as people is ignored.[116]

A major empirical work on the workers of the world, Silver's *Forces of Labor*, alluded to above, concludes on a note similar to Castells's:

> there is no reason to expect that just because capital finds it profitable to treat all workers as interchangeable equivalents, workers would themselves find it in their interests to accept this. Rather, insecure human beings (including workers) have good reasons to insist on the salience of non-class borders and boundaries (e.g., race, citizenship, gender).[117]

While the best-sellers of Hardt and Negri, like those of Žižek, testify to the continuing creativity and attractiveness of Marxist traditions, sociologically minded readers at least are likely to be sceptical of the former's invocation of Spinozan claims that 'prophetic desire is irresistible' and that 'the prophet can produce its [sic] own people'.[118]

A Resilient Left

The recent trajectory of Marxism also includes a mode of resilience, cutting its path through thickets of adversity across an altered, unmapped terrain. The London-based *New Left Review*, having become the generally recognized

---

116. M. Castells, *The Information Age*, vol. 3, 346, italics omitted.
117. B. Silver, *Forces of Labor*, 177.
118. M. Hardt and A. Negri, *Empire*, 65.

flagship of left-wing social thought, at least in the Anglophone world – and in fact *hors pair* in other language areas, including in the francophone and hispanophone worlds (there is now a Spanish edition, which joins its Italian, Greek and Turkish stable-mates) – successfully relaunched itself in 2000 with a manifesto of intransigence, of 'uncompromising realism'.[119] Perry Anderson, the guiding spirit of the *NLR* for more than forty years as well as the pilot of the relaunch, is not only a major Marxist historical scholar but also a master of intellectual critique, and is capable of applying those critical powers to Marxism itself.[120]

Historically, the *NLR* might best be called a neo-Marxist journal, always keen on theoretical innovations, with a muted enthusiasm for straight political economy and plainly uninterested in exegesis and concomitant polemics. Brilliance and radicalism have been the *NLR* criteria for publication, never orthodoxy of whatever kind. This comes at a price of short-term political insignificance, although the journal has always cultivated contributions from and on radical social movements, from the student movement of the 1960s to the *altermondialiste* movements of the 2000s. And *NLR*'s outspoken political radicalism has not prevented its being included in the Social Science Citation Index.

Some other important mouthpieces of European Marxism have also survived – above all, three German publications, *Das Argument, Prokla* and *Sozialismus* (originally entitled 'Contributions to Scientific Socialism'), which have yet to confront a generational succession; but also the British journal *Capital and Class*. The

119. P. Anderson, 'Renewals', *New Left Review* 2: 1, January–February 2000, 14.
120. P. Anderson, *In the Tracks of Historical Materialism*, London: Verso, 1983; *A Zone of Engagement*, London: Verso, 1992; *The Origins of Postmodernity*, London: Verso, 1998.

philosophical-feminist couple Wolfgang Fritz and Frigga
Haug still direct *Das Argument*, and the economist Elmar
Altvater guides *Prokla* (an acronym for 'Problems of Class
Struggle'). More generally intellectual or directly politically
oriented journals have been more vulnerable. The French
Les Temps Modernes survived the death of Sartre and de
Beauvoir but is no longer a major Left publication. The
once very lively British publication *Marxism Today* folded
with the ending of the Soviet Union. In Italy, the *Rivista
del Manifesto* gave up in 2004.

New journals have also been started up, often with
powerful publishers' backing. *Historical Materialism* is put
out by the Dutch academic publisher Brill in Leiden. The
American-based *Rethinking Marxism* is published by
Routledge, which is now also taking over the relaunched
(although still under its old editor) late Cold War anti-
Soviet journal *Critique* as a 'Journal of Socialist Theory'.
American Cold War survivors *Monthly Review* and *Science
and Society* have also weathered the American victory. The
originally British annual *Socialist Register* is now edited
from Toronto. Even France has a couple of postcrisis
journals, such as the banner-flying, philosophically
oriented *Actuel Marx*.

Insofar as they have soldiered on, the European
Communist parties and their successors have mostly
shown little intellectual Marxist resilience. Most of the
Eastern European ex-CPs have situated themselves well
to the right of Scandinavian social democracy. The once
largest Western European CP, the Italian, has, as we
have noted, recently broke with social democracy to
embrace plain 'democracy'. The innovative and self-
critical East German former PDS and its Rosa Luxemburg
Foundation, however, do retain some commitment to
Marxism, as do the two remaining 'orthodox' parties, the
Greek and the Portuguese.

The Great Encyclopaedia of resilient Marxism is the
Historisch-Kritisches Wörterbuch des Marxismus, directed by

the Haugs and published by *Das Argument* in Hamburg, in cooperation with the Free University of Berlin and the Hamburg University of Economics and Politics. In its high-level intellectual doggedness, the Dictionary is a unique exemplar of the refusal to surrender. Conceived in the 1980s and launched in 1994, it is planned to extend to some fifteen or more volumes. Although largely a German project, its eight hundred collaborators include Étienne Balibar, Pablo González Casanova and other international figures. It has a bilingual website: www.hkwm.de. Volume 6, which appeared in 2004, took us up to 'Justice'. At its planned two-year pace, the project will be completed in 2022. 'Marxism' here is not only understood in its broadest ecumenical sense, but also read across a wide sociocultural register. To take some random examples, there are entries on Brecht, double-work and *Dummheit in der Musik* (stupidity in music).

The 1990s also saw an ambitious attempt at an exegetical 'reconstruction' of Marx's critique of political economy, Moishe Postone's *Time, Labor and Social Domination* (1993), and a valiant and pedagogical defence of dialectical thinking by another American, Bertell Ollman's *Dialectical Investigations* (1993).[121] Postone's reading takes the concepts of value and commodity one level of abstraction further from socio-economic analysis, into a conception of social domination – reminiscent of Max Weber's 'iron cage' of rationalization – which 'subjects people to impersonal, increasingly rationalized structural imperatives and constraints that cannot adequately be grasped in terms of class domination . . . It has no determinate locus.'[122] As

---

121. Ollman has continued his dialectical teaching into the new millennium, now provided with a choreography of dialectical investigation, *Dance of the Dialectic*, Urbana, IL: University of Illinois Press, 2003, 169.
122. Postone summarizing his own book, 'Critique and Historical Transformation', *Historical Materialism* 12: 3, 2004, 59.

commercial evidence for a resilient interest in Marxism, one might also cite the multivolume 'Retrospective' on Marx and his work put out by Routledge in the 1990s, of which the eight volumes on Marx's social and political thought, edited by Bob Jessop, are the most pertinent here.[123]

A monumental document of resilience, though of less than encyclopaedic format, is the *Critical Companion to Contemporary Marxism* (2007),[124] almost eight hundred pages long, put out by the journal *Historical Materialism* and edited by the French philosophers Jacques Bidet and Stathis Kouvelakis. Bidet has made another large-scale attempt at a 'reconstruction' of Marxism, on the basis of the dual market- and organization-based 'matrix of modernity'. The *Companion* has a predominantly French philosophical tone – and is published with subsidies from the Ministère française chargé de la culture, in spite of being put out in English in the Netherlands – but covers a wide ground, mainly of textual explication and contemporary intellectual history. Its most interesting contribution is a detailed, albeit not explanatory, overview by André Tosel of the recent fate of Marxism, as philosophical theory and as scholarship, in Italy and France.

Individual examples of resilience are plentiful and, once again, extend across a far wider disciplinary field than that of social theory. But two deserve to be added to this inevitably partial and limited selection. Among the few political survivors of the French *événements* of 1968, Daniel Bensaïd is a leading Trotskyist cadre and the author of the well-written *Marx for Our Times*. On the other side of the Channel, Alex Callinicos is probably the most prolific

---

123. B. Jessop and C. Malcolm-Brown, eds, *Karl Marx's Social and Political Thought*, 4 vols, London: Routledge, 1990; second series, Bob Jessop and Russell Wheatley, eds, London: Routledge, 1999.
124. Brill: Leiden.

of contemporary Marxist writers, with a wide-ranging philosophical, social and political bibliography.[125]

In a recent, somewhat unsystematic collection of autobiographies by sociologists of the 1960s cohort, two in particular, by Michael Burawoy and Erik Olin Wright, keep the banner of Marxism flying.[126] Burawoy, an incisive, theoretically driven ethnographer of work, and Wright, the no less theoretically driven researcher of class structures, have also signalled a joint project to build 'sociological Marxism'.[127] How far this will develop in practice remains to be seen, but as a plan it is the most ambitious scholarly project of resilient Marxism, with great potential. While innovative in intention – 'building' – its reassertion of the Marxist political agenda as well as its core analytics, minus the theory of value, makes 'resilient' a more apt epithet here than 'neo'. Burawoy and Wright's sociological Marxism has an explicitly normative as well as scientific commitment, linked to 'the political project of challenging capitalism as a social order'. Its sociological core is the concept of class as exploitation, with a research agenda that follows from a theory of 'the contradictory reproduction of contradictory class relations' – essentially, a Marxian analysis of capitalism and its political and ideological institutions, though shorn of the original's historico-philosophical wrapping. Intrinsic here is the assumption that the capitalist dialectic is still operating, though in a somewhat smoothed-over fashion:

First, the dynamics of capitalist development generate changes in technology, the labour process, class

---

125. As a small sample, see, for example, A. Callinicos, *Against Postmodernism; An Anti-Capitalist Manifesto; The Resources of Critique*, Cambridge: Polity, 2006.
126. A. Sica and S. Turner, eds, *The Disobedient Generation*, Chicago: University of Chicago Press, 2005.
127. Burawoy and Wright, 'Sociological Marxism', 459–86.

structure, markets, and other aspects of capitalist
relations, and these changes continually pose new
problems of social reproduction ... Second, class
actors adapt their strategies in order to take advantage
of the weaknesses in existing institutional arrange-
ments. Over time, these adaptive strategies tend to
erode the ability of institutions of social reproduction
to effectively regulate and contain class struggles.[128]

Reproduction is especially problematic and conflictual for
class relations: 'Social relations within which antagonistic
interests are generated will have an inherent tendency to
generate conflicts, in which those who are harmed will try
to change the relation in question.'[129] Instead of going on
to demonstrate the power of this programme, the authors
veer off into one of their pet utopias, the 'universal basic
income'; but that should not detract from the immense
value of their concise, concrete and jargon-free restatement
of Marxism as a contemporary science. While aware of
the implications attendant upon a nineteenth-century
'ism', Burawoy and Wright retain it as a marker of
belonging to and continuing a tradition.[130]

LOOKING AHEAD

What emerges, first of all, from this overview is the uneven
effect of the broken triangle of classical Marxism – politics,
social science and philosophy. In the North Atlantic region
(and the rest of the world is not so different, with a few
local exceptions in Indo-Latin America), Marxist politics
has either disappeared or become completely marginalized;
at best, as a sympathetic observer of Kerala, Tripura or

128. Ibid., 473.
129. Ibid., 474.
130. Ibid., 460n.

West Bengal might put it, it has been suspended. The socialist horizon, bright red just three decades ago, has vanished.

On the other hand, left-wing intellectual creativity has not ceased. Its greatest moments may have passed: not only the moment of Marx and Engels, but also that of the Second International, from Kautsky to Lenin; of Western Marxism from Lukács to Gramsci; of Eastern and Southern Marxism from Mao to Mariátegui; even the more recent moments of Althusser, Bourdieu and their different national equivalents. But there is much more of an intellectual Left production today than, say, forty or fifty years ago. The left-wing generation of the 1960s, particularly of those radicalized before the romantic moment of 1968, has not surrendered. The value of the thematic changes in discourse, noted above, is debatable, but they do not appear to be promising objects of denunciation. The existing repertoire of positions is unlikely to please everyone, but it does nevertheless include rallying points for nearly everybody on the Left.

However, formative generational experiences tend to have enduring effects, and this writer's critical distance is, of course, suspect. His views are those of someone from the 1960s generation, writing about his contemporaries, about his comrades or former comrades. What about the prospects ahead?

Capitalism still produces, and will continue to produce, a sense of outrage. To that extent, a line of continuity from the nineteenth through the twentieth and twenty-first centuries will remain, in resistance as well as in critique. Coming philosophers are almost certain to publish new readings of Marx. Twenty-first-century anti-capitalist resisters and critics are unlikely to forget the socialist and communist horizons of the past two hundred years. But whether they will see the dawn of a different future in the same colours is uncertain, perhaps even improbable. New cohorts of anticapitalist social scientists will certainly emerge, and many will read Marx, but it may be doubted whether many will find it meaningful to call themselves Marxists. The classical Marxist triangle has been broken and is most unlikely to be restored.

The resilience of the 1960s Left spans an important historical caesura. This was the generation that lived both the peak of working-class strength in developed capitalism and the beginning of its decline. It saw both the image of revolution, in 1968, and the implosion of the revolutionary perspective in 1989–91, a perspective that had opened up in 1789 and 1917. In the interim, it experienced the genuine sex and gender revolution of the late twentieth century. It was the generation which lived through, and criticized, the climax of North Atlantic capitalism and which went on to witness the return of East and South Asia to the front stage of the world.

For contingent, practical reasons – space/time availability and linguistic limitations – this overview has been confined to the North Atlantic/North American area. That is still the base whence the most deadly bombers and missiles take off, but it is no longer the chief front on which the destiny of capitalism in the twenty-first century will be decided. Hence the extraordinary importance of global theorizing and, even more, of global empirical investigations.

The new radical *élan* of Latin America awaits its major analyses. From the cross-fertilization of domestic place-holding Indian Marxism and the 'postcolonial' creativity of South Asia's brilliant intellectual diaspora should come something which rises to the level of the region's rising importance and intriguing complexity. The small left-wing Chinese intelligentsia has the incomparable advantage of a front-row seat for the current turn of world history. These are sources from which invaluable contributions can be expected to spring, not only towards better understandings of the world but also towards perspectives of change.

In the current situation, a certain *defiant humility* seems to be the most adequate intellectual stance. Defiance before the forces of capital and empire, however powerful. Humility before the coming new world and the learning and unlearning that it will call for.

Index

Locators in *italics* indicate illustrations.

Democratic Front for the
  Liberation of Palestine
  (DFLP), 53
Democratic Party (Italy), 161
Democratic Party of the Left
  (Italy), 161
Derrida, Jacques, 164, 166
Desai, Meghnad, 164
Descartes, René, 73
Deutscher, Isaac, 99
development, 16, 37
developmentalism, 37
DFLP (Democratic Front for
  the Liberation of Palestine),
  53
Dialectical Investigations
  (Ollman), 175
Dialectic of Enlightenment
  (Horkheimer and Adorno),
  70, 78, 83
dialectics, 108–10
Discourse on Method (Descartes),
  73
Dobb, Maurice, 99

Eagleton, Terry, 133
East Asia, 18
East Asian outward-development
  model, 8–11
Eastern Europe, 47–48, 91,
  96–97, 162
Eclipse of Reason, The
  (Horkheimer), 78
*Economics of Global Turbulence,
  The* (Brenner), 154
economies, political, 108, 153–57,
  175, 180
Ecuador, 45
Edwards, John, 46
Einstein, Albert, 112
empire, 113
Empire (Hardt and Negri), 132,
  152, 169
employment, 18–19

Encyclopédie, 122
Engels, Friedrich, 38, 67, 68,
  71, 117
enlightenment, 27, 58–59, 60,
  67, 71
environmentalism, 31–32, 37
Envisioning Real Utopias
  (Wright), 135–36
Eros and Civilization (Marcuse),
  78
Europe, 47–49, 130–33, 143,
  159, 174
  See also Eastern Europe;
    Western Europe
European Left, 159
European Marxism, 96, 97–101,
  173
evangelicalism, 21

Fanon, Frantz, 105
feminism, 22–23, 94–95, 149–51
feu sacré, Le (Debray), 131
Finance Capital (Hilferding),
  89–90
Fogarasi, Bela, 83–84
Forces of Labour (Silver), 145, 172
For Marx (Althusser), 99
France, 96, 98, 112
Frank, Andre Gunder, 103, 140,
  145
Frankfurt School, 70, 72, 82–84
Fraser, Nancy, 167
French Revolution, 27, 143
Friedmann, Georges, 93
Fritz, Wolfgang, 174
'From the Class Struggle to the
  Struggle without Classes'
  (Balibar), 142
fundamentalism, 20–21
futurism, 134–40

gender, 149–50
*General Theory of Exploitation
  and Class, A* (Roemer), 156